FINDING THE

PEACE
GOD
PROMISES

FINDING THE
PEACE
GOD
PROMISES

An updated edition of *The Peace God Promises*

ANN SPANGLER

ZONDERVAN

Finding the Peace God Promises
Copyright © 2011, 2014 by Ann Spangler

Previously published as *The Peace God Promises*

Requests for information should be addressed to:
Zondervan, 3900 Sparks Dr. SE, Grand Rapids, Michigan 49546

Zondervan titles may be purchased in bulk for educational, business, fundraising, or sales promotional use. For information, please email SpecialMarkets@Zondervan.com.

ISBN 978-0-310-32014-2 (softcover)
ISBN 978-0-310-34057-7 (ebook)

Library of Congress Cataloging-in-Publication Data

Spangler, Ann.
    The peace God promises: closing the gap between what you experience and what you long for / Ann Spangler.
      p. cm.
      Includes bibliographical references (p .).
      ISBN 978-0-310-26715-7 (jacketed hardcover)
      1. Peace—Religious aspects—Christianity. I. Title.
  241'.4—dc22   2011010953

Cover design: Curt Diepenhorst
Cover photo: Hofhauser / iStockphoto®
Interior design: Katherine Lloyd, The DESK

Printed in the United States of America

For Sandy Vander Zicht,
with gratitude

CONTENTS

ACKNOWLEDGMENTS

F ew books if any come into being simply because an author wills them to. This book would not have been possible without the help of many others. Thanks to Dudley Delffs, former trade book publisher at Zondervan, for his support for this book and for his suggestions regarding the shape it might take. Executive editor and associate publisher Sandy Vander Zicht has been both my friend and my editor throughout most of my writing life. Her prayers, insights, and encouragement have made all the difference. I am grateful for her sharp editorial eye and her unstinting efforts to help make this a better book. Thanks also to Tom Dean, senior director of marketing for trade books at Zondervan, and his team for their efforts to reach the broadest possible audience. Curt Diepenhorst did a wonderful job designing the cover. I also want to express my gratitude to Linda Kenney for acting as my agent for this book. I have greatly appreciated her encouragement, counsel, and support through many years.

Several editors at Zondervan pointed out helpful resources for exploring the peace that comes from belonging to a vital community. So thanks to Katya Covrett, Bob Hudson, Ryan Pazdur, Sandy Vander Zicht, and Verlyn Verbrugge for help with this topic. A special thanks to Verlyn for his editorial help on the first edition and the revised edition of this book. I'm grateful also to

Andrea Doering for sharing the story, told in chapter 7, of her brave quest to carve out a day of rest for herself and her family. The Reverend Jack Roeda first mentioned the concept of the "non-anxious presence" and suggested it as a line of enquiry for the book.

Lois Tverberg, my mentor regarding the Jewish roots from which Christianity has grown, graciously agreed to review a draft of chapter 7 and made several helpful suggestions. She also introduced me to the work of David Pileggi, rector of Christ Church in Jerusalem, whose insights into the Jewish world of Jesus are both helpful and fascinating, and to Joseph Telushkin, a Jewish spiritual leader and writer who has many helpful things to say about Jewish ethics, including the ethics of speech. Certain of his insights are incorporated into chapter 11.

Mark Buchanan is both a client and a friend, and he is also one of my favorite authors. So it is no coincidence that his influence is evident throughout the book. In addition, I want to particularly acknowledge the work of Miroslav Volf. His book *The End of Memory* greatly influenced my understanding of the difficult topic of how memories of wrongs suffered can be dealt with in redemptive ways.

As always, my assistant, Barbara Adams, has provided invaluable help in tracking down quotes, obtaining necessary permissions, and making corrections to various drafts of the text. Her patient and cheerful support is a consistent blessing, which I do not take for granted. I am also indebted to Linda Bieze, Leslie Dennis, Joan Huyser-Honig, and Patti Swets for their prayers on behalf of the writing of this book. Week after week the persistent prayers of these women, who are like sisters to me, buoyed me and kept me moving forward.

Lastly, I am grateful to Lori Vanden Bosch for her skillful, sensitive work on the revised edition of the book. She has the gift of never letting a multitude of trees obscure the forest. That was crucial in reorganizing the manuscript.

Any deficiencies in the book, of course, can only be credited to my account. Whatever these may be, I hope that on balance this will be a book that will draw many people to a life of greater peace.

Chapter 1

WHERE'S THE PEACE?

I have no peace, no quietness; I have no rest,
but only turmoil.

Job 3:26

S everal years ago, I began thinking about how I would celebrate a milestone birthday when it was yet a ways off. As the mother of two young children, I longed for a little peace, for time to get away from the incessant demands that children inevitably make. I wanted to do what I wanted to all day long for an entire week with no one tugging at me, no one needing me, and no one making any demands.

A full two years before that birthday, I decided I would celebrate on some island paradise. Perhaps the Cayman Islands. Just thinking about it made me feel more relaxed, anticipating the warm sand caressing every step, the blue-green water stretching out to the horizon. One year out, I thought it might be more practical to plan a trip to Florida. There are lots of gorgeous beaches in Florida. Six months in advance of my significant birthday, I set my heart on a weekend in Chicago. Then, a week before the big day, I thought, "If only I could get out to the mall!"

IF ONLY!

For most of us, the word *peace* has a certain wistfulness to it, an "if only" quality.

> "If only I could go on a vacation."
> "If only I could get a better job."
> "If only I had married someone who was easier to get along with."
> "If only my kids would listen."
> "If only I could retire."

This sense of wistfulness arises because we can think of countless things that prevent us from experiencing the peace we desire.

Each of us can come up with our own list of "if onlys"—of the situations or the people we would like to change so that our lives wouldn't feel so rushed and anxious and stressful. Such lists, of course, imply that peace is situational. We will experience peace once our troublesome circumstances are resolved, once that difficult person moves on, once we find a new job. Circumstances do, of course, affect our sense of happiness. But what happens when our circumstances remain frustratingly the same, as they so often do? Can we still find the peace God promises? Or are we the grand exception, the one person to whom his promises do not apply?

Perhaps you are reading this book because you wonder what life would be like if you could find a way to banish your anxiety or to let go of the peace-destroying thoughts that plague you. Or maybe you are hoping to rid yourself of memories that control and disturb you. Or perhaps you are sure you will explode if one more thing gets added to your harried schedule. Whatever the circumstances, you want the peace God promises to become more evident in your life.

There was a time in my own life when I thought (but did not admit) that money would make me feel secure. At other times, I was sure life would calm down if only I could find a way to exert more control over my circumstances and the people who were causing me difficulty. Perhaps you've been drawn to other strategies, building your life on the assumption that peace will come as soon as you find the perfect relationship, the perfect vacation, the perfect job. Of course there's nothing wrong with a good vacation or a great job. And finding someone who loves you is one of life's great gifts. All of these can add happiness to your life. But none is capable of producing the peace God promises.

The problem is not so much that we are searching for a kind of peace that does not exist, but that we are looking for peace in the wrong places. It's like searching for New York City in Florida. No matter how many times you drive from Jacksonville to Key West, you will never find it.

MY QUEST FOR PEACE

All of us come to our longing for peace from slightly different places. I confess that one of my least favorite Scripture passages is from 1 Peter. In it, Peter urges the Christians of Asia Minor, specifically the women, to develop a "gentle and quiet spirit" (1 Peter 3:4). This has always rubbed me the wrong way, perhaps because, though I am neither loud nor brash, I would not characterize myself as particularly gentle. And why, I wonder, does Peter address only the women? Are men off the hook then, free to behave in rough and brutish ways? Couldn't a case be made that men in particular have a need to reign in their aggressions?

I have been tempted to conclude that Peter preferred women who were passive and weak rather than strong and confident. Such a preference would seem to fit the stereotype of some Middle Eastern males even today. But is that entirely fair? I have recently begun to wonder whether I have been misreading the advice Peter was giving the early Christians. What if, instead of urging them toward weakness, Peter was urging them toward strength, saying, in effect, that they were capable of becoming people whose peace was so strong that it radiated a kind of steady calm to everyone around them?

As I have thought about Peter's advice concerning a gentle and quiet spirit, I have realized that some of my own worst interactions, especially with my children, have happened when I have felt anything but gentle at the core of my spirit. Instead of radiating calm, I fear I have sometimes radiated anxiety in the form of nagging comments, irritation, or anger. In the light of such self-recognition, gentleness and the peace from which it springs suddenly begin to look more appealing.

A few years ago, my youngest came to me in tears. When I asked what was wrong, she told me through sobs, "I'm not going to be able to go to college."

"But, honey, you're only ten. Why are you worried about college?"

"Because you're always complaining about money. I know you won't be able to afford it. What am I going to do?"

I was stunned to hear the level of anxiety that had gripped my ten-year-old. Why was she agonizing over whether she would be able to go to college? Then it hit me. She had merely been absorbing my own frequently voiced anxieties about the economy, albeit drawing the wrong conclusion.

And then there was my eldest. How had she and I gotten into the practice of yelling whenever we couldn't see eye to eye? Was that the kind of atmosphere I wanted to pervade our home, to characterize my heart? Surely there must be a way for my children and me to take hold of the peace God promises to those who follow him.

My need to become a more peaceful parent has been my own entrée to the subject of peace. I want to stop worrying so that I can help create an environment where trust and faith can grow. This is what makes me want to explore what the Bible means when it talks about peace, especially as it applies to the human spirit. Are there disciplines, ways of living that lead to peace? And conversely, are there ways of looking at the world and responding to it that lead to anxiety and a conflicted life? This book represents my search for answers to these questions. I approach the topic not as an expert, nor as someone who has mastered the things that lead to peace, but as a fellow explorer, drawn to the subject because of my own need. As such, this is not primarily a book about world peace but about personal peace, which can in turn affect the wider world in which we live. To quote Wendell Berry, "One must begin in one's own life the private solutions that can only in turn become public solutions."

Obstacles to Peace

Though I approach the subject with my own needs in view, I realize that others will be drawn to it from different directions.

You may, for instance, be sensing your need to repair a strained relationship. Or perhaps you have been frustrated by past hurts that will not heal. Or maybe you are bothered by the pace and insecurity of modern life. You want to find ways of both slowing down and calming down.

There are, of course, countless obstacles to discovering the peace we seek. For instance, though we live in the richest nation on earth, many of us are plagued by financial insecurity. During the recession, I confess to having had many sleepless nights, wondering if my life savings were going to be washed away by an economic tsunami. How would I send my children to college; what if I couldn't pay the bills; how could I follow the biblical injunction to tithe when business conditions were so depressed? I wish I could tell you that I have come through with flying colors, trusting God to provide. But that would not be entirely true. Nor perhaps would it be true of many others who have lost far more than a good night's sleep. Is it possible to experience peace even in the midst of so much tension and difficulty?

And what about psychological ills like anxiety and clinical depression? Though medicine and therapy may help, they cannot always vanquish our fears.

Remember the classic movie *Psycho*? I have a friend who refuses to take a shower if she is the only one home, just in case Norman Bates happens to be in the neighborhood. Apparently, she isn't alone in her fears. Here's what a few more self-confessed neurotics had to say about taking showers. Their comments are posted on a website entitled "I am neurotic."

If I am home alone and decide to take a shower, I get really scared that someone will break into my house and kill me when I'm naked and vulnerable. To keep this from happening, I sing different genres of songs in the shower (rap, show tunes, country). I do this in hopes that the killer will enjoy one of these types of music and decide against killing me.

Second post:

I have the same fear, but I get out of the shower, while it is still running. This way, anyone waiting for me to finish won't know I am actually out of the shower. Then with a towel securely wrapped around myself, I take the stick from my loofah and quickly open the door ready to attack. Just in case, I have the element of surprise on my side.

Third post:

If you are singing country, it still might get you killed.

From the number of additional responses to the initial posting, it seems clear that on any given night there must be thousands of people belting out songs in the shower, not because they are feeling carefree, but because they are desperately hoping to scare off a serial killer! We laugh at the stories of these self-confessed neurotics, but neuroses are anything but funny for those who suffer from them.

FEARS AND PHOBIAS

Many years ago I began to develop a phobia about flying. I started to dread getting on a plane. This was a problem since my job at the time involved a great deal of travel. The slightest turbulence would result in sweaty palms and a racing heart. One day as I was fearfully flying across the country, I felt God nudging me.

"What are you afraid of?"

"Of crashing and dying."

"And then what would happen?"

"Well, I would be with you."

"Then what are you afraid of?"

As this discourse was proceeding, another thought came into my mind: *Perfect love casts out fear.* I had always interpreted this passage from Scripture (1 John 4:18) to mean that once I attained perfect love, I would no longer experience fear. It suddenly occurred to me that God himself embodies perfect love. His love could cast out my fear. So I asked him to remove the fear of flying from my life, to push it out with his presence so there would be no more room for it in my mind. Immediately, I felt a sense of peace, and the phobia I had been developing was stopped in its tracks. Since then I have had occasional bouts of fear during a rough flight, but nothing that could be called phobic.

Why do I tell you this? At least in part to assure you of my credentials as a person in search of peace. Also to give you permission to examine your own fears in light of God's grace and the peace he wants to extend to you.

Fear, of course, is a natural emotion. When it is operating properly, it can help us survive threatening circumstances. None of us, for instance, should feel comfortable strolling down the road with a tornado in sight. Our fear helps us do the prudent thing—in this case running for dear life toward shelter or lying facedown in a ditch. But fear that has metastasized into generalized anxiety or that has grown to phobic proportions is neither natural nor helpful. Such fears can cripple our relationships and poison the future as well as the present.

Fear also has a mysterious power of attraction; that is, it can draw the very thing we're afraid of into our lives. I remember the moment I encountered the famous quote from Franklin D. Roosevelt's first inaugural address: "The only thing we have to fear is fear itself." I was still a child, but I thought it sounded like nonsense. I knew there were things to fear — a snake might bite you, a car might run over you, your mother might die. I didn't understand that Roosevelt, quoting Francis Bacon, was trying to rally people in the midst of the Great Depression, warning them about fear's destructive power. He knew that financial panic could result in financial ruin. Our fears can attract what we fear the most.

STRESS AND DEPRESSION

Like fear, stress is also a normal part of life. But the pace of modern life has made stress levels skyrocket. Several years ago, an Amish newspaper was deluged with hundreds of letters from people wanting to know how to become Amish. Many of these people were looking for a way to opt out of modern society in order to pursue what they saw as a more peaceful life, little realizing that living with Amish austerities might produce its own kind of stress for those unused to them.

Though modern Western societies have produced many marvelous things, they have not generally produced cultures conducive to developing a sense of personal peace. Little wonder that the Swahili word for "white man" — *mzungu* — literally means "one who spins around."

Robert Sapolsky, professor of biology and neurology at

Stanford University, points out that prolonged stress "can wreak havoc with your metabolism, raise your blood pressure, burst your white blood cells, make you flatulent, ruin your sex life, and if that's not enough, possibly damage your brain."

So much for the good news.

What about those of us who suffer not only from prolonged stress but from depression? It is impossible, of course, to quantify such suffering. Fortunately, medication and therapy can be tools God uses to bring us to a place of greater peace. But medication has its limitations. Though it can ease and sometimes erase our suffering, it cannot ultimately extend to us the kind of peace that God is promising.

RECLAIMING PEACE

Etty Hillesum was a Jewish woman who wrote about peace in one of the least peaceful moments of her own relatively short life. Imprisoned by the Nazis during World War II, she perished at Auschwitz on November 30, 1943. Though she could have gone into hiding, avoiding the fate of millions of Jews, she refused, choosing instead to "share her people's fate." A year earlier, in September of 1942, she wrote this diary entry:

> Let me just note down one more thing for myself: Matthew 6:34: "Take therefore no thought for the morrow: for the morrow shall take thought for the things of itself. Sufficient unto the day is the evil thereof.—"
>
> We have to fight them daily like fleas, those small worries about the morrow, for they sap our energies. We make mental provisions for the days to come, and

everything turns out differently, quite differently. Sufficient unto the day. The things that have to be done must be done, and for the rest we must not allow ourselves to become infested with thousands of petty fears and worries, so many motions of no confidence in God ... Ultimately, we have just one moral duty: to reclaim large areas of peace in ourselves, more and more peace, and to reflect it towards others. And the more peace there is in us, the more peace there will be in our troubled world."

That is the mission of this book, to help us reclaim large areas of peace in ourselves so that there will be more peace in our troubled world. In doing so, we too will have to fight the infestation of daily fears and worries, the continual "motions of no confidence in God," replacing them with the peace that comes from resting in the character of God.

The chapters that follow explore various dimensions of the peace God offers us. Part 1 looks at the source of our peace, God himself, and examines the role of each person in the Trinity in addressing our heartfelt need for peace. Part 2 looks at the vital spiritual practices that help us to connect to God and access his peace. Part 3 examines the situations that most deeply challenge our peace, including suffering and strife. And Part 4 reveals how we can pursue faith in our daily life through practical disciplines such as exercise, simplicity, and gratitude.

A small book on a large topic, *Finding the Peace God Promises* won't tell you everything you want to know about peace, but it may well get you started on a journey that will change your life. If yours is anything like mine, progress on that journey may be sometimes hard to measure. You may even feel as if you are taking one step forward and two steps back. Like life itself, our progress toward peace does not follow a linear path. But as you base your peace on the character and personhood of God— Father, Son, and Holy Spirit—you will find that in the end, even the least peaceful times in your life will have drawn you closer to the one who is himself our peace. The mystery of how exactly this can happen resides not so much in our own efforts but in God's grace and in his unswerving desire to deliver on the promise he has made.

Pursuing Peace

1. Many of us believe that peace depends on our circumstances. "If only" we had enough money, enough time, enough patience, then we would feel peaceful. What are some of your "if onlys"?

2. What is driving your personal quest for peace? What obstacles—such as fear, stress, or depression—stand in the way?

3. Etty Hillesum said, "Ultimately, we have just one moral duty: to reclaim large areas of peace in ourselves, more and more peace, and to reflect it towards others. And the more peace there is in us, the more peace there will be in our troubled world." How might you reclaim peace in your life?

Part One

PEACE IN GOD — FATHER, SON, AND HOLY SPIRIT

Grace and peace be yours in abundance.

1 Peter 1:2

Chapter 2

WHERE PEACE
COMES FROM

*He will keep in perfect peace all those who
trust in him, whose thoughts turn often to the
Lord!*

Isaiah 26:3 LB

A friend once told me about a professor he knew who was so absent-minded that he drove to a city for a meeting and then afterward grabbed a cab to the airport when the meeting was over. Another time, while standing next to his car in a college parking lot with an armload of books and a puzzled look on his face, the professor hailed a student, saying, "Excuse me. I wonder if you could tell me—am I coming or am I going?"

When it comes to our spiritual lives, some of us are similarly challenged. We don't really know whether we are coming or going. Caught up in everyday events, we fail to remember not only that we are headed somewhere but that we are traveling a path with Someone. Staying close to that Someone—to God our Father—is vital to living a life of peace. Otherwise, we will become so invested in life here and now that we will forget our purpose for living. Remember the story of Dorothy, the young girl from Kansas, who followed the yellow brick road in search of the Emerald City and the great wizard of Oz? At one point in her quest, she and her companions wander into a field of poppies. Though Dorothy doesn't know it, she is standing on dangerous ground because the flowers exude a scent that can lull unwary travelers into a sleep that will last forever. Our own world can sometimes function like that gorgeous field of poppies, lulling us by its pleasures and seducing us by its comforts. After a while, we are tempted to settle down. A nicer house, a better job, a thinner body—these and a thousand other desires can command our thoughts, our talents, and our energy. We get caught up with countless desires, stuck like Tar Baby to all our wants.

Trouble, too, can become a snare. The stock market plunges and fear proliferates. Our children struggle and anxiety takes over. Our career disappoints and depression sets in. If you wonder whether this might apply to you, think for a moment about the things that upset you most in the past week. Then about the things that have given you the most joy. Do any of them have the whiff of eternity about them, or do they merely carry the scent of this world? Our emotions can provide clues to what is driving us. Is the power and presence of God the driving force of my life, or am I constantly buffeted by the winds of success, comfort, fear, or anxiety?

Both desires and struggles, if pursued or resisted without reference to God, can be a fog obscuring not only the path ahead but the fact that we are even on a path. At times, they make us forget where God is leading us. Of course God can use our difficulties to advance his plans. It is sometimes true, as the saying goes, that the obstacle itself is the path. A sickness can lead to deeper prayer and greater empathy. A difficult child can lead to greater faith and patience. Nothing is wasted in the lives of those who belong to God. Even our desires can help us discern his will. The mistake comes from pursuing or resisting desires and difficulties on our own, without seeking God's help and guidance.

If we want to experience peace, it is vital to stay on the path, to continue to follow the one who loves us.

WHATEVER HAPPENED TO *SHALOM*?

We know that the world's original harmony was wrecked by sin. Like a Molotov cocktail thrown into a backyard garden, sin exploded the world that God had made, fracturing and dividing it. Instead of wholeness, brokenness; instead of health, illness; instead of friendship with God, alienation; instead of peace, strife.

Because we live in this fallen world that is yet to be fully redeemed, we can only glimpse the fullness of God's peace. Scripture tells us, however, about God's original intentions for the world he made. Consider the Hebrew word *shalom*, which is often translated "peace" in English translations of the Bible. Comparing the word *peace* to the word *shalom* is like comparing a twig to a log or a boy to a man. When we think of peace, we tend to think of an inner sense of calm or an absence of conflict. *Shalom*, however, means these things and more. It means "wellness," "completeness," "perfection," "safety," "soundness," "success," "wholeness," "health," and good relationships between people and nations. When there is *shalom*, everything is as it should be, our lives are as God meant them to be, our world is in the order he intended.

To experience peace in its fullness is to experience healing, satisfaction, prosperity. To be at peace is to be happy, fulfilled. It is a sign of the blessed life of the new creation. Peace has a whiff of paradise about it. It offers us a taste of the world to come.

Sometimes we sense this kind of peace as we worship with others, or as we pray quietly, or when forgiveness is asked for and received. *Shalom* is life as it should be. Bent things are straightened. Hurt things are healed.

The Bible, however, locates *shalom* in only one place—in God himself. Early in the history of his people, God instructed Moses to extend this blessing to them:

> The LORD *bless you*
>   *and keep you;*
> the LORD *make his face shine on you*
>   *and be gracious to you;*
> the LORD *turn his face toward you*
>   *and give you peace. (Numbers 6:24–26)*

We find peace by living in harmony with God. As we do, our divisions, both external and internal, start to heal. We become fulfilled, complete. The harmony we have with him in turn produces harmony with others and harmony within ourselves.

I admit that I have yet to meet anyone who seems perfectly at peace. But I do know some who seem closer to that ideal than others. Mr. José is the janitor at my daughter's school. Even without a high status job he is one of the most admired men I know. Parents and students love Mr. José because he is kind to even the most difficult children. The peace he radiates helps set the tone for the entire school.

I know a pastor and his wife who have experienced extraordinary things in their ministry. Whenever I hear about their next venture, my stomach begins to churn because of the risks they take. I have watched them as they have listened to God and then made decisions that can't possibly work unless God comes through. And he does come through in remarkable ways. Maybe you know people like that, people who are able to take on challenges with an underlying sense that no matter what happens, God is still with them.

Remembering God

David Pileggi, rector of Christ Church in Jerusalem, points out that Judaism is a religion of remembering. The Israelites are to remember that they were once slaves in Egypt, whom God delivered with a mighty hand and an outstretched arm. They are to remember how he led them in the desert for forty years. They are to remember the Sabbath day and keep it holy.

So important is the command to remember that God instructed the Israelites to do something that sounds strange to modern ears. He told them to sew tassels on the hems of their garments. Why? First, because clothing, then as now, reflected a person's social status. In Egypt the Hebrew slaves had occupied the bottom rung of society. By commanding his people to attach tassels to the hem of their garments, God was elevating their status, treating them like royalty because tassels were generally worn by princes and kings, not by common people and certainly not by slaves. He was reminding them who they were: his precious chosen people.

Second, the hem symbolized a person's identity and authority. It was common for a man to "sign" a legal contract by pressing the hem of his garment into the clay tablet on which that contract was engraved. So whenever the Israelites looked at the tassels on their hems, they remembered two things: first that they belonged to God as his chosen people, and second that they were obligated to keep his commandments.

The Jewish people, Pileggi says, are called to remember so that they can obey. Why, he asks, do observant Jews wear a *kippah*, or *yarmulke*, today? To remember that there is a God in heaven. Why do they kiss a *mezuzah*? Because inside this small, oblong box attached to the doorposts of their homes is a copy of the *Shema*, the prayer that begins: "Hear, O Israel: The LORD our God, the LORD is one" (Deuteronomy 6:4).

Remember, remember, remember—this is the echoing refrain that trails God's people throughout their history. To forget is to be driven into exile, to be expelled from God's presence. To remember is to live with him in the Promised Land.

THE "O" WORD

Remembering God involves more than thinking about him or having warm feelings toward him. Remembrance, as I alluded above, involves the dreaded "O" word. It involves *obedience*. For the Jews, remembering involved obeying the law that God had given on Mount Sinai.

But let's be honest. Most of us aren't thrilled when we hear the phrase "God's law." To many of us, talk of religious laws conjures the prospect of legalism, of being bound to a life of rigid rules and regulations. While English translations of the Bible translate the

Hebrew word *torah* as "law," Jewish translations often render it as "teaching" or "instruction." So if we think about what transpired on Mount Sinai, it makes sense to think of it as the moment when God gave his people vital instructions for their journey. Without these instructions, they would never have reached the Promised Land. God was teaching them to become his followers, people who stayed close to him and did not stray. To obey would bring them great happiness. To disobey would bring them great pain. Rejecting God's guidance would mean losing the fulfilling, vibrant life to which he had called them.

Why did the Israelites need instruction or guidance? Because they had entered into a relationship with God, and being in relationship always involves some kind of requirements. Students, for instance, have to be willing to learn from their teachers. Spouses have to love and serve each other. Friends have to be loyal. If these requirements aren't met, the relationship will deteriorate.

Since this is true of human relationships, why should we be surprised to learn that being in relationship with a holy God also has its requirements? Belonging to God and enjoying his fellowship means that we give up the desire to be our own god. Belonging to him means that we are called to listen and do what he asks. It means that we love what he loves—justice and mercy and goodness. We are to be holy even as he is holy. That was God's purpose for drawing his people out of Egypt in the first place. He wanted not just to free them from their captors but to love them and live in their midst.

So God chose Israel to belong to him in a special way, and Israel became holy. He gave them the gift of becoming his people. But the gift, as David Pileggi points out, requires "maintenance."

Imagine for a moment that someone has just given you a very

expensive gift—the car of your dreams. For me that would be a 1957 Thunderbird. It would have a supercharged V–8 engine, fourteen-inch wheels, and a removable hard top complete with portholes. It would also be starmist blue. Now that would be a gift to cherish—and to care for. While I do not mean to equate our relationship with God to a vintage sports car, I do want to make the point that the priceless gift we have been given in God needs to be maintained. We maintain it by closely following his instructions and his teaching regardless of how we feel at any given moment.

God says, "You shall not steal," so you don't cheat people even when you feel backed into a corner. God says, "Honor your father and mother," so you show respect whether or not your parents deserve it. God says, "You shall not commit adultery," so you don't sleep with someone just because you are in love. God says, "You shall have no other gods before me," so you cherish his ways instead of bowing down to the idols of our era—political correctness, money, sex, power. As Pileggi says, "The gift is free, but the maintenance is costly."

A CAUTIONARY TALE

So we know that God's law contains instructions for the good life, the blessed life. Sadly, however, merely *having* the instructions doesn't help us to *keep* the instructions. As a cautionary tale of sorts, look at what happened to the Israelites. While God was giving Moses the tablets of the law, they were busy making a golden calf to worship. With Moses gone and God apparently absent, they were quick to fill the leadership void with a false god of their own making. Despite all that had happened to them—the destruction of their enemies, the guidance through treacherous deserts, the daily provision of manna—they were quick to forget, ready to complain. They didn't like the fact that following God meant embracing things they disliked, things like obedience and waiting. Instead, they defaulted to a longing for the familiar, for comfort and luxury. "If only we had meat to eat!" they cried. "We remember the fish we ate in Egypt at no cost—also the cucumbers, melons, leeks, onions and garlic" (Numbers 11:4–5). Remembering what was predictable, safe, and comfortable in Egypt, they had forgotten the terrible cruelty they suffered there.

A WAY OUT OF DISTRESS

But what does the story of the forgetful (and yes, rebellious) Israelites mean for us? It means that anyone who wants peace has to make a personal and conscious decision to remember God and to obey him. We have to choose to leave behind the world and all its troubles and seductions, to leave behind the bondage that comes from living without God. You leave when you forsake your old life and decide to follow God.

But leaving is not easy. Some of us are afraid of what God might ask, of what he might require. We prefer a life of predictable bondage to one guided by an unpredictable God. Others resist leaving because they fail to recognize their chains. They know they have problems, but life does not seem so bad. Why should they throw it all away to embrace a life that requires them to live by faith and not by sight? Even those who are eager to leave Egypt may be tempted to return as soon as life becomes difficult—or as soon as life becomes easy!

A friend in graduate school once told me how Christ had made himself known to her. She was to the point of killing herself when something happened to convince her that God was real and that he cared about her. By the time I met her, Robin had been a Christian for some time. A few years later I learned that she no longer considered herself a Christian. What had pulled her off course? I don't know, but I suspected it was a man she had met. A lonely girl who had never had a boyfriend, the lure of that relationship may have seemed more appealing than the faith she had once embraced. Proverbs 14:12 cautions us with these words, "There is a path before each person that seems right, but it ends in death" (NLT).

Like the Israelites and like my friend, some of us have faltered on our journey out of Egypt. Perhaps we have encountered obstacles that diverted us. Our fellow travelers, others who profess to love Jesus, may have disappointed us. Plans we thought God would bless did not turn out well. Prayers we prayed were not answered as we had hoped. We may have begun by making small compromises that grew into larger ones. Hurt by another's sins, we grew bitter. Afraid we might run out of money, we stopped giving. Seeking a little pleasure to soothe us, we got hooked on drugs or pornography. Or perhaps we merely said a series of small "no's" to God that have hardened into a way of life bereft of his presence. Before we know it, we are no longer following but retreating—headed back to Egypt, back to a place of bondage, boredom, forgetfulness, and despair.

If that describes you, even in part, there is still time to turn around, still time to get back on the path. Fortunately you don't have to find your way back all on your own. For the Father has sent his Son to go looking for you. Jesus is the good shepherd who leaves the ninety-nine sheep in search of the one that is lost. You have only to ask for his help.

The word that describes this act of turning around, of leaving the wrong path in order to get on the right path, is *repentance*. It is the first step in our journey back to God. As Eugene Peterson points out, "Repentance is a realization that what God wants from you and what you want from God are not going to be achieved by doing the same old things, thinking the same old thoughts. Repentance is a decision to follow Jesus Christ and become his pilgrim in the path of peace."

Peterson goes on to say that repentance "is the action that follows the realization that history is not a blind alley, and guilt not an abyss. It is the discovery that there is always a way that leads out of distress—a way that begins in repentance, or turning to God." Repentance is the vital first step out of a life of trouble and despair. Repentance moves us closer to the only true source of peace: God himself.

How Peace Was Lost

A glance at Genesis reveals the paradise of peace that God intended from the beginning. Genesis 3 depicts God walking in the garden in the cool of the day. In the beginning Adam and Eve had easy access to their Creator. Because of their relationship with him, they enjoyed perfect peace—a sense of wholeness, well-being, completeness, safety, and health. Words for sickness, confusion, pain, and death hadn't even been invented because no one had ever experienced these things. But then something tragic happened—or failed to happen. They failed to listen, failed to trust, failed to follow. Instead they went their own way. And their choice to head in another direction led them in the worst direction of all—straight into exile. Being cast out of paradise, they ended up living in a land of thistles and thorns.

Though the human race experienced a tragic fall from grace, we know that God has not given up on us. Revelation tells us that at the end of time, after the smoke has cleared, we will see God face-to-face. And when we see him, we will experience the perfect peace for which we long. Nothing we need, nothing we desire, will be missing—not one thing. That's the end game. Knowing God. Going to God. Seeing God, not "only a reflection as in a mirror," as Paul characterized the way we currently see (1 Corinthians 13:12). The goal is to see God clearly, to have what has been called the "beatific vision," an experience that will transform our eternity. Now we catch glimpses of God, then we will see him as he is.

But God is shy. He inflicts himself on no one and recedes from those who will not follow him. Or perhaps he is not shy but merciful, unwilling to indulge our error by blessing us with his presence. Maybe he withdraws, hoping we will turn back and follow him closely once more, desperate for his presence and eager for his peace.

Until we see God face-to-face, the peaceful life is not about ease. It's not about finding the perfect relationship. It's not about collecting all the treasures and gadgets we can stuff into our pockets. It's not about turning back or settling down. It's about keeping to the path until we reach our final destination in the arms of God.

Pursuing Peace

1. In the *Wizard of Oz*, Dorothy and her friends nearly forget their quest because they wander into a field of poppies that lull them to sleep. What are the things in your own world that make you forget the purpose God has for your life?

2. What is the meaning of *shalom*? What does that tell you about God's plan for this world?

3. How does remembering and obeying God bring us peace?

Chapter 3

PEACE IS
A PERSON

*But he was pierced for our transgressions, he
was crushed for our iniquities; the punish-
ment that brought us peace was on him, and
by his wounds we are healed.*

Isaiah 53:5

One day a father was sitting in his study, attempting to work
while keeping an eye on his young son. Looking around
for something to occupy the boy, he tore a picture of the earth
from the pages of a magazine. Ripping the picture into small
pieces, he cupped the shredded blue and green papers in his hands
and offered them to the boy as a gift. "Here's a puzzle for you to
put together," he said.

Trotting out of the room to reassemble the puzzle, his son
seemed happy with his new assignment. Turning back to his work,
the father smiled, confident that at last he could count on some
uninterrupted work time. But his sense of satisfaction vanished a

short time later when the boy walked back into his study, trium-
phantly announcing the successful completion of the puzzle. "How,"
the surprised father asked, "did you put it together so quickly?"

"It was easy," the boy replied. "There's a person on the other
side of the page and when you put the person together, you put
the world together."

The boy's unintended wisdom cuts to the heart of our quest
for peace. Peace is not found in a place. Peace is not found in this
world. Peace is found in a person—in Jesus.

A TURBULENT LIFE

The world loves the peaceful Jesus: the Christmas baby in the
manger, the wise and humble teacher of the Sermon on the Mount.
Gentle Jesus meek and mild ... or so we think. But a careful reading of the Gospels reveals someone who seems at times to go out
of his way to provoke his listeners. If Jesus was such a great man
of peace, why did his life generate so much turbulence? Why was
he murdered? Why is there still so much controversy about lifting
up his name in public?

Matthew's gospel tells of a pivotal moment in Jesus' ministry.
It happened when he called his disciples together, giving "them
authority to drive out impure spirits and to heal every disease
and sickness" (Matthew 10:1). What an incredible day that must
have been for twelve ambitious men. It was what they had been
waiting for—the dramatic action that would inaugurate the coming kingdom. When Jesus took his rightful place on the throne,
they would be elevated to positions of power. Surely it was time
to break out the champagne!

But Jesus said otherwise. He was not sending them to a party,
nor was he launching a victory march. Instead, he was sending

his disciples out like sheep among wolves. Brother would betray brother, fathers would turn against their children, and children would rebel against their parents. Any semblance of peace would be destroyed. "Do not suppose," he said, "that I have come to bring peace to the earth. I did not come to bring peace, but a sword" (Matthew 10:34). Jesus refused to make peace with the status quo. He would not paper over the world's ills. He intended, instead, to overthrow the reign of sin and death in order to restore the world to God. His mission then and now is to bring nothing less than true *shalom* to those who belong to him.

No wonder there is such fierce opposition to the gospel! That's why we who are called by his name should also expect turbulence. Promising his disciples that they would be hated because of their allegiance to him, Jesus reminded them that a "student is not above the teacher, nor a servant above his master" (Matthew 10:24). But those who would lose their lives for his sake, he said, were the ones who would find life.

Recently I heard a story about a lawyer I'll call Elena Sanchez. She works as a consultant for AJS, a Christian human rights agency in Honduras whose primary purpose is to secure justice for people who cannot secure it for themselves. In October 2010, Sanchez was abducted and forced into a taxi by two men who said they had been hired to execute her. Over and over they grilled her:

"Who pays you?"

"Do you work for AJS?"

"Are you investigating SETECH?"

Sanchez had not, in fact, been targeting this private firm in the course of her investigation. What she had been doing was looking into allegations that various governmental agencies with ties to private industry were complicit in the systematic violation of employees' rights.

Weeks earlier, a man employed by the Secretary of Labor had asked her the same question: Was she investigating SETECH? Though Sanchez assured him her investigation was not focused on any one company, the man persisted, saying, "Stand up and look out that window. Down there in the street is where you always take a taxi when you leave here, and it would be so easy to put an end to you with a few bursts of gunfire. It wouldn't be desirable for you to end up thrown away into a thicket."

Now here she was riding in a taxi with two thugs who were threatening to kill her. When she refused to answer their questions, one of them spit out a vulgar epithet and said, "We're asking you a question, answer it." Aware that another lawyer had been gunned down four years earlier in the midst of a case that did involve SETECH, Sanchez was terrified. She prayed fervently that the men would release her.

Then something strange happened. All of a sudden, the two men became frightened, claiming they could not move their hands. Unable to explain what was happening, they instructed the cab driver to alter his route. Forty minutes after forcing Elena into the taxi, the men suddenly ordered the cabbie to stop in front of a hardware store. Then they told Sanchez: "Get out now, and may God protect you."

Sanchez is still in danger, which is why I can't use her real name. But I assure you the story is real. How do I know? I heard it from someone who works for AJS in Honduras, a man I trust. He and his Honduran colleagues have taken the words of the prophet Micah seriously, "What does the LORD require of you? To act justly and to love mercy and to walk humbly with your God" (Micah 6:8). They know that walking humbly with Jesus is not a cakewalk. And indeed, it can lead to a turbulent and even dangerous life.

THE PROMISE OF PEACE

So what kind of peace does Jesus promise, if not a peaceful life? Listen for a moment to the promises Jesus makes to us in Scripture:

> "Peace I leave with you; my peace I give you. I do not give to you as the world gives. Do not let your hearts be troubled and do not be afraid." (John 14:27)

> "I have told you these things, so that in me you may have peace. In this world you will have trouble. But take heart! I have overcome the world." (John 16:33)

Did Jesus really mean it when he said these things? If so, what kind of peace was he talking about? And what exactly did he mean when he spoke of "my peace" and of giving it "not as the world gives"? Furthermore, how could Jesus say these things on what must have been the most troubled night of his life? Just a short while later he would fall on his face in Gethsemane, praying to his Father about the fearful events that would soon overtake him. To his lethargic and prayer-less disciples, Jesus described his soul as being "overwhelmed with sorrow to the point of death" (Mark 14:34). He knew, though they did not, that in just hours he would suffer arrest, abandonment, and death. How, then, could he speak of peace and of having so much of it that he could give it away?

The very first words Jesus speaks to his disciples after his resurrection, when they are gathered together, are these: "Peace be with you!" (John 20:19, 21), as if he knows precisely their need, terrified as they are by the Romans and by the religious leaders who conspired to murder their rabbi. They are in profound turmoil because everything they believe has been called into question by his death. Was Jesus only a foolish dreamer and they his gullible disciples?

The Hebrew phrase Jesus probably used to greet his astonished friends was this: *Shalom aleikhem*—"Peace be upon you." This is the traditional greeting by which many Jews still greet each other today. But instead of wishing his disciples peace in an ordinary, everyday kind of way, Jesus was actually delivering peace in person. Noting the wounds in his hands and side and seeing him alive again, his disciples would have known that this was no dreamer. Truly he was the long-awaited Messiah. This shocking realization must have produced in them a new and deeper kind of peace, one they could never have imagined.

PEACE IS NOT AN EMOTION

The Gospels use the Greek word *eirene* for "peace." One commentator says that peace "is a state of being that lacks nothing and has no fear of being troubled in its tranquility; it is euphoria coupled with security." I don't know about you, but I would gladly settle for a little bit of "euphoria coupled with security." But is this what God promises in the here and now? History does tell of martyrs who went to their death gladly and peacefully. And Paul, writing from prison, says that he has "learned the secret of being content in any and every situation" (Philippians 4:12). Paul is saying that it is possible to learn to be peaceful regardless of our circumstances.

Still, it would seem that even Jesus did not always experience emotional peace. Witness his anger at the way the temple had been turned into a marketplace, or his tears at the death of his friend Lazarus, or his agony in the garden of Gethsemane. Perhaps neither Jesus nor his Father are promising that we will always *feel* peaceful, at least while we are here on earth. Maybe they are more concerned that we learn to base our lives on the peace that Christ has won, experiencing ever-deepening *shalom* as we follow after him.

That peace has been won by the person we know as the Prince of Peace, or in Hebrew *Sar Shalom*. Though Jesus spoke of bringing a sword, he also brought *shalom* to all who embraced the gospel.

- To the woman bleeding for twelve years, he said: "Daughter, your faith has healed you. Go in peace and be freed from your suffering." (Mark 5:34)
- To the woman who washed his feet with tears, he said: "Your faith has saved you; go in peace." (Luke 7:50)
- To the disciple who doubted, he said: "Peace be with you!... Stop doubting and believe." (John 20:26–27)
- To his disciples before his death, he said: "My peace I give you." (John 14:27)

In these scenes and many others from the Gospels, we see Jesus restoring what is broken, healing what is bent, saving what is on the brink of destruction. If we want peace, we must embrace the one who brings it. Living as his disciple is the only way to experience all that Christ has for us.

Let's turn again to the words Jesus spoke to his disciples on the night before his death: "Peace I leave with you; my peace I give you. I do not give to you as the world gives. Do not let your hearts be troubled and do not be afraid" (John 14:27).

Peace in our world is usually won and maintained by military might. But the peace Jesus offered his disciples is a different kind of peace, extended in a different kind of way. It is a peace obtained, not by a show of power but by an apparent show of weakness—Jesus died on a cross like a criminal and outcast. By virtue of his love and his obedience to the Father, Christ achieved a peace that only he could win. Because he was divine and human, he was the only one capable of representing the interests of both a holy God and sinful humanity.

It is this peace that Jesus was extending to his disciples the night before his death. Like a father who realizes his children will be shattered the moment he is taken from them, he tries to reassure them that, in the end, all will be well. Because Jesus lived out a perfect obedience to the Father, we can have peace with God, and that peace can be the unshakeable foundation on which our own lives are built.

CHOOSING A SCHOOL

How does the peace Christ offers get worked out in a life? Let me offer a small example. Recently my daughter and I were trying to determine the best high school for her to attend. For the past nine years, ever since kindergarten, she had attended a small neighborhood school, a place that enfolds children in its welcoming embrace. With only fifteen students in her graduating class, it had been a great place to learn and grow. But now it was time to venture out into the big, wide world of high school. Most of her friends were heading to a relatively small school a few miles away. But for a variety of reasons, this didn't seem like the right choice for her. I prayed and we discussed the options. Together, we decided on another school.

As the fall of her freshman year approached, I found myself wavering, worrying about how large my daughter's new school was. It was so big, I told friends, that new students would need a GPS to find their way around. What if it was just too much of a change? Or what if she had a hard time making new friends since many of the students would already know each other, coming as they did from feeder schools? As my anxiety rose, I began reconsidering the decision, thinking that perhaps it would be safer to opt for the school her friends were planning to attend. But what about the guidance I believed God had given? Remembering the prayer that had shaped our decision, I decided to stay the course.

Though she's had to adjust to the new school, my daughter loves it. What's more, the high school she would otherwise have attended has encountered some unexpected difficulties, with the result that some of her friends are now transferring to other schools.

Most of our lives are lived in the midst of everyday concerns. Though my anxiety caused me to wobble a bit along the path, God gave me the grace to stick to it. Because of that, my daughter and I are experiencing more peace in the present. Following Christ may not always feel peaceful, but doing so will create openings for his *shalom* to characterize our lives.

FOLLOWING THE RABBI

Borrowing a phrase from Friedrich Nietzsche, Eugene Peterson wrote a book entitled *A Long Obedience in the Same Direction*. It's a phrase that captures our call as followers of Christ. In the Jewish world of Jesus, it was customary for disciples to follow their rabbi so closely that they got covered in the dust from his footsteps as he walked up the sandy path ahead of them. They wanted to hear every word, to understand every instruction, to stay close to their rabbi as he led the way. Spending hour after hour, day after day, following him around, they not only listened to what their rabbi said. They watched what he did and the way he reacted. Their goal was to become as much like him as possible because they believed he was living a life that pleased God. That's how we should think about our relationship with Christ. Jesus is our Rabbi, the one who shows us what it means to live the God-blessed life. Remember his words to his disciples: "I am the way and the truth and the life. No one comes to the Father except through me" (John 14:6).

My brother Jim has a way with dogs. We call him the family dog whisperer. In addition to curing our pets of their various neuroses, he has helped other people's dogs, guilty of bad behaviors like peeing on rugs, jumping on people, running away, pulling on leashes, leaping through screens, barking nonstop, and fighting with other dogs. Jim tailors his approach to the dog's temperament, seeking to understand its strengths and weaknesses. But his secret weapon, the thing that helps the dogs to change, comes from the fact that he knows dogs are pack animals in search of a strong pack leader. Without one, dogs often become anxious, neurotic, or aggressive. So he becomes their pack leader. Once the dogs sense that he has taken this role, they begin to calm down and get into line. They no longer have to try to be their own pack leader. Sensing his energy, they become both peaceable and teachable, and it is amazing how well they get along with each other and how quickly they change.

Though humans are not dogs, we too need a leader whose energy can lead us toward greater peace and freedom. When we follow Jesus, our Rabbi, and stay close to him, we begin to calm down. We become more peaceful because we let go of our pretensions to rule the universe. We stop trying to do the impossible, such as seeing the future or controlling every circumstance. We leave what belongs to God in God's hands. We also listen for his voice because we know that Jesus can help us navigate our present. Following him makes us peaceable and teachable, even in the most unpredictable and frightening of circumstances. Don't believe me? Consider the story of Peter after the crucifixion of Jesus.

PETER: FROM TERROR TO COURAGE

Peter huddled with the other disciples behind a door bolted hard against their fear, wondering whether the religious leaders who had crucified Jesus might soon be coming for them. But instead of the terror and despair that had filled him for the last two days, he felt a growing sense of calm in the midst of a new excitement.

He had been at the tomb that morning and had seen the strips of linen lying on the ground. He had encountered the risen Lord. Now men had just come from Emmaus claiming they too had met the Lord.

Suddenly, Jesus appeared, a smile lighting his face as though he had just returned from a short trip. "Peace be with you," he said (John 20:19). Then he held out his hands, inviting Peter and the other disciples to examine his wounds. Finally he asked for food. Watching him eat filled Peter with wonder.

Then Jesus said it again: "Peace be with you! As the Father has sent me, so I am sending you" (John 20:21).

By now Peter was beginning to get the message. He remembered what Jesus had said to the crowd: "Blessed are the peacemakers, for they will be called children of God" (Matthew 5:9). Jesus was telling him to get going, to spread the good news, to tell everyone about the peace Christ offers.

After the resurrection Peter was transformed. No longer cowering in fear, he proclaimed the message of the gospel fearlessly. Like Peter, we are to receive the peace God promises with joy, and then we're to go out and share it.

Fortunately, Jesus has given us a helper to guide and enable us, saying: "I will ask the Father, and he will give you another advocate to help you and be with you forever—the Spirit of truth. The world cannot accept him, because it neither sees him nor knows him. But you know him, for he lives with you and will be in you" (John 14:16–17). When Jesus appeared to Peter and his disciples in that startling visitation after his resurrection, he breathed on them, saying, "Receive the Holy Spirit" (John 20:22).

If God the Father is our source of peace, and God the Son provides access to that peace through his sacrifice on the cross, God the Holy Spirit is the one who enacts, enables, and empowers our peace. If we want to experience the peace God promises in ever deeper measure, we need to be vitally connected to the Holy Spirit—to God's presence on earth.

PURSUING PEACE

1. What kind of peace does Jesus promise?
2. What might your life look like if your daily goal was to be "covered in the dust" of the rabbi, Jesus?
3. How has this chapter and the life and words of Jesus upended your traditional understanding of peace?

Chapter 4

PEACE IN
THE PRESENCE

> *For the kingdom of God is not a matter of*
> *eating and drinking, but of righteousness,*
> *peace and joy in the Holy Spirit.*
>
> Romans 14:17

A few years ago, when the economy was more robust, I got sidetracked. It wasn't drugs, it wasn't sex, but it was money. I fell in love with a yellow cottage in an upscale development surrounded by a white picket fence. This development beat anything in the area, with a sparkling pool in the middle of a beautiful patio from which you could gaze at boats passing to and fro in the channel on their way to Lake Michigan. I didn't buy it to live in but as an investment. I figured I could rent it out on a weekly basis in the summer, helping to pay the mortgage. The stock market had been a treacherous environment for some years. Why not diversify and put some money into real estate? So I did.

This decision wouldn't have been so bad except that I did it even though I had a check in my spirit, a niggling feeling that this wasn't what God wanted me to do with my money. I prayed about it, hoping the feeling would fade. But it didn't. Yet I felt sure that anyone familiar with the development would congratulate me for making an astute investment. So I went ahead with the purchase. Shortly after that, the stock market collapsed and the real estate market plunged to levels that hadn't been seen since the Great Depression. The tidy profit I had envisioned from selling the property in a few years time began looking more like a significant loss. I felt the weight of it daily—and still do.

What had seemed like God's disapproval when I was considering the purchase began to look much more like God's concern. He hadn't given me peace about buying the property because he knew exactly what lay ahead. What if, instead of trying to kill my joy, the Lord had been trying to preserve it, knowing that owning this property would not add to my sense of peace and security but subtract from it? It's embarrassing to disclose this episode in my life. I'd rather not write about it. But it's such a good illustration of what happens when we ignore the promptings of the Spirit. If you suspect God of being a Grinch or a killjoy, it will be difficult to follow when he heads off in a direction you don't want to go. But if you know the kingdom of God is about righteousness, peace, and joy in the Holy Spirit (Romans 14:17), why wouldn't you want to listen?

GIVING SWAY TO THE SPIRIT

Belonging to Christ means that we give sway to his Spirit, who dwells within us. The Spirit not only directs us but enables our obedience, reshaping us into "little christs," followers who are eager to do God's will and seize the opportunities he gives us. The more we learn to live in the Spirit, the more peace and joy we will have, and the more fruitful our lives will become.

In her book *Practicing Peace*, Catherine Whitmire tells the story of William Dizler, a man who lived in the nineteenth century. It seems that Dizler sensed that God wanted him to use part of his lunch hour to stand near an open window and read the Bible aloud. He did it for several weeks until he suddenly felt that he didn't need to do it any longer. Sometime later, a clergyman from a local church came to visit him. "I feel I should tell you of an experience of one of my parishioners," the pastor explained.

Dizler asked if it was anyone he knew.

"I think not," the pastor replied. "She was a young girl who lived in an upper room across the courtyard from your office. Although she knew she was dying of tuberculosis, she had become bitter toward God and refused to meet with me. Then one day, the voice of an unseen, unknown reader came to her. She tried not to listen. She put her hands over her ears and pulled up the covers. Still the voice came day after day. Gradually she began to listen and she died in great peace."

Dizler could have dismissed the thought that he should spend the better part of his lunch hour reading Scripture out loud in front of an open window. It might have seemed like a silly thing to do. But instead, he listened and a young woman found peace.

SHARING THE PEACE

The Holy Spirit gives each of us opportunities to follow his promptings. But he doesn't force us to take hold of them. I remember driving north to visit my elderly uncle shortly after my aunt had died. He lived alone in a small cabin, an idyllic but lonely place. I was concerned about him, knowing that his health was failing and that he had few friends and family close by. I wondered about the state of his soul. As far as I knew, he had never shown the least bit of interest in any kind of religion, nor had his wife, my aunt. Shortly before she died, I'd had the chance to pray with her and talk to her about Christ's love. Now I wanted to talk to him, but I was having difficulty working up the nerve. We had never had a serious conversation about anything. Yet my conscience kept nagging me. What if he were to die without my ever having said anything about what Christ meant to me?

So I forced myself to drive up to see him. The closer I got the more uncomfortable I became. Soon after I arrived, I found myself awkwardly launched into a conversation about faith and about Jesus and about how different my life had become since I surrendered it to him. It was an inelegant presentation. I cringed inwardly, thinking how clumsy and inept my words must sound. But to my surprise, my uncle warmed to the conversation, saying he had recently come to know God's love and that he could feel God's presence with him.

Even the old black dog that lay by his side, he said, was a sign that God had been watching out for him. The dog had wandered in one day, sick and lost. My uncle had nursed him back to health, and now the old dog and the old man had become great companions. I don't remember everything we talked about, but by the time I left, I felt peaceful about my uncle's well-being. I don't know that my words made a big difference. But I believe my obedience mattered. At the very least, having that conversation with my uncle gave me peace, and it gave God another opportunity to show his love to my uncle.

A NON-ANXIOUS PRESENCE

Early in their seminary training, many pastors-to-be learn a curious phrase. Their professors instruct them that they are called to be a "non-anxious presence," that is, the one person in the room who maintains a peaceful presence when everyone around them is losing it. When a child has died, when a couple is on the verge of divorce, when someone is in despair, when the church is threatening to split, they are to be present in a way that reorients the emotional and spiritual atmosphere. Their leadership can make all the difference. But this, of course, is far easier said than done. Here's how one woman dealt with her own anxiety while trying to help a family in crisis.

Amy Butler had spent an anxiety-filled day at the hospital with parents whose child had died in utero. Now they were waiting for their baby to be delivered. Refusing to leave despite her inability to ease their suffering in any significant way, she tells what happened when she was allowed to hold the infant in her arms shortly after the baby was born: "I finally felt my anxious pastoral presence easing when I got to hold that just-born baby. He was a precious little guy, perfectly formed; wrapped in a blanket, warm and solid in my arms. After hours of anxious anticipation I felt at that moment nothing anxious at all ... just the calm assurance that this baby is surely loved by his parents and by God. Strangely enough, as we cried and prayed and said goodbye it seemed to me that all of us around that hospital bed had stumbled unexpectedly upon a few holy moments, an oasis of grace, a true, almost tangible, enveloping *non-anxious presence*.

"After this week of poignant opportunities to try to be a *non-anxious presence* in situations that make me hyperventilate when I just think about them," she observed, "I'm starting to suspect that this *non-anxious presence* we learned about in seminary is not the pastor's presence at all. What our task as pastors must be, I got to thinking, is not necessarily to BE the non-anxious presence but rather to WELCOME that non-anxious presence precisely because when we step into situations like that we *are* so anxious. Most days the best we bring is the expectation of *God's* pastoral, *non-anxious presence*—not our own."

Amy Butler's story is an encouragement to all, but to especially those of us who find it hard to maintain our own sense of calm in difficult circumstances. Once again, staying vitally connected to the Holy Spirit will not only increase our peace but it will help us to become channels whereby that peace can spread to others.

BECOMING A PEACEFUL PERSON

Edwin Friedman was an ordained rabbi, a family systems counselor, and a leadership consultant who focused on leadership, not as a system or technique but as a way of thinking and being. Friedman defined *presence* as "the trail of confidence, poise, bearing, calmness, focus, and energy one leaves wherever one goes ... Presence has to do with emotional maturity, the willingness to take responsibility for one's own emotional being and destiny." Without "presence" a person cannot lead. Even if you are not in a leadership position, learning about maintaining a "non-anxious presence" can help you bring peace to others, whether in the workplace, at church, or at home.

Instead of becoming enmeshed in the emotional atmosphere, getting sucked in by the frustration, fear, or anger that may be swirling around them, mature people are able to maintain their equilibrium. They tend to solve problems not by trying to fix others but by focusing on how they can improve themselves. For instance, instead of instructing people to "stay calm" in a difficult situation, they put their energy into remaining calm themselves. Even one such leader at the helm of an organization can turn the tide.

According to Friedman, the task of mature leaders is to bring more of their self into the workplace. By doing so, they can help other members of the organization grow in maturity. They do this by staying calm, maintaining their connection to key people in the organization, and challenging those they lead whenever it is appropriate to do so.

Friedman believed that the most effective leaders, whether at home or at work, adapt to strength rather than weakness. Instead of reshaping the organization in reaction to its least mature members—the chronic complainers, the underperformers, and the overly dependent—they are able to tolerate a certain amount of pain in others because they know it provides an opportunity for people to grow. "If one family member can successfully *increase* his or her threshold for another's pain," he commented, "the other's own threshold will also increase, thus expanding his or her range of functioning."

But shouldn't good parents and effective leaders be empathetic, able to relate to people's weaknesses as well as to their strengths? In fact, Friedman believed that empathy is the least effective way to improve a family or an organization. Why? Because empathy is an adaptation toward weakness. Friedman wasn't advocating cold-hearted, disconnected leadership styles. He knew that the dual task of a leader was to maintain a sense of calm *while* staying connected to others in the organization. He wasn't advising leaders to distance themselves from others. Quite the contrary. His point was that too much empathy impedes growth.

What does any of this have to do with Jesus, the Holy Spirit, or us? A look at how the Gospels portray Jesus reveals that Jesus was the master of the non-anxious presence. Sleeping in the boat in the midst of a storm, feeding the five thousand with a few loaves of bread, raising a dead girl to life despite the taunts of those who thought it couldn't be done—Jesus was often the one peaceful person in the room. He was also the one who consistently challenged his disciples to lives of greater maturity. Remember that Jesus didn't promise his disciples an easy life. "In this world you will have trouble," he assured them. "But take heart! I have overcome the world" (John 16:33). Jesus gives us a hope that is grounded in him and empowered by the Holy Spirit. As Paul writes to the Romans, "May the God of hope fill you with all joy and peace as you trust in him, so that you may overflow with hope by the power of the Holy Spirit" (Romans 15:13). Trusting in Christ and relying on the Spirit, we cannot help but overflow with the joy, peace, and hope that God provides.

The peace that counts, the peace that is real, is the peace that emanates from our relationship with Christ, not from the fact that our circumstances at any given moment happen to be favorable or pleasant. As we grow in his likeness and are transformed by his Spirit, we begin to experience his peace in greater measure.

Spreading Peace at Home

So how can we spread the peace of the Spirit in our own lives? As someone who has been both a mother and a business manager working in settings that have ranged from moderately healthy to downright dysfunctional, I know it is often easier to maintain a non-anxious presence in the workplace than it is at home. Home is where we are most invested. We want our children to thrive, our spouses to do well. It's easy to become anxious and frustrated when problems arise. Home is also the place where we disclose who we are, dropping the pretense we try to maintain in public. It may be easier to keep our cool in a place where everyone else is trying to keep theirs. Family relationships can also be tangled and complex, adding to the tension we feel.

If you've been a parent for even five minutes, you know how easy it is to give in to the child who whines the loudest or complains the most. But effective parenting means that we need to endure our own discomfort at the same time that we allow our children to experience a measure of discomfort themselves. We have to do what's right for our children regardless of how uncomfortable their resistance makes us feel. So if one child, for instance, is good at helping around the house while another never wants to lift a finger, you don't let the second child off the hook, doing her work for her or shifting the burden to the sibling who works without complaint. Being able to act rightly while remaining calm will increase our effectiveness as parents. Even if we don't feel peaceful, we can sometimes pretend to be calm, thereby increasing the chance for positive outcomes now and in the future.

Let me offer a personal example. You may remember that what prompted me to write this book was my sense that some of my worst interactions, particularly with my children, were created by my anxiety. I wanted to find a way of relating to them with more peace and less stress. When I began learning about Friedman's work, I started to wonder what our family would be like if I could regularly display the kind of non-anxious presence he describes. What if I were to stop overreacting to my children's emotions, instead finding a way to stay vitally connected to them while maintaining a sense of calm? Perhaps I could, as he advocates, learn to "delegate anxiety" by leaving the appropriate responsibility with them.

For instance, instead of nagging my daughter about her homework, I could simply indicate that the decision of whether to do homework belonged to her as did the subsequent consequences should she choose not to. I've tried that approach and am happy to report that it often works. It may seem like a small thing, but this simple act of delegation has reduced the tension in our home.

Friedman's description gave me a target at which to aim and some tools for becoming less anxious. Learning more about his work also made me wonder whether I was overdoing it in the empathy department, adapting more to my children's weaknesses rather than to their strengths. Now that I recognize the pattern, I am doing my best to step back so that my children can step up.

As Friedman points out, sometimes the most effective way to lead can be to decide that we will *not* meet another person's needs. Attempting to meet every need is a recipe for anxiety because none of us can meet every need perfectly. Such misdirected efforts also create more anxiety because they deepen dependency, preventing others from successfully rising to the challenges they face. Of course this dynamic holds true in our spiritual lives as well. God allows us to face certain challenges because he knows it is the only way we will grow—both personally and even as a society.

"NOTHING SHORT OF THE HOLY SPIRIT"

One woman who embodied non-anxious leadership and impelled a whole society to grow was Elizabeth Fry, a nineteenth-century Quaker. Fry had heard about the appalling conditions of women inmates at Newgate Prison in the center of London. Inside the prison, 190 women and 100 children were housed together—prostitutes, murderers, and professional thieves alongside innocent women and children who had merely fled abusive homes. None of the inmates were given bedding or clothing, with the result that many were living in nearly unbearable conditions.

Fry had been warned that the prison was dangerous to enter. Those who made the mistake of straying too close to the iron grating separating the crowd of prisoners from the rest of the world would often find themselves in the steely grip of grimy hands thrust through the grating and holding them fast. Scratch marks on their faces were the only mementos of their unlucky encounter with those on the other side of the prison gate.

Despite the danger, Elizabeth Fry was determined to enter the women's section of the prison. She did so for the first time in January 1817. As a crowd of shrieking women surged toward her, Fry held her own, calmly explaining that she was a mother who wanted to know how to help the prisoners and their children. To the astonishment of the prison guards, the inmates halted their furious attack and listened carefully to what Fry had to say.

Later Fry formed a volunteer organization of women dedicated to feeding, clothing, educating, and praying with the inmates and their children. Through her work she sparked a worldwide prison reform movement, something that might not have happened without the empowering presence of God. She also set up a nurses' training school that influenced Florence Nightingale, the woman credited with laying the foundation for professional nursing. Fry knew that her work depended on God's guidance, remarking that "nothing short of the Holy Spirit can really help forward the cause of righteousness on earth."

GUIDED BY THE SPIRIT

Like Elizabeth Fry, we may be called to exhibit God's peace in a dangerous or turbulent setting. Needless to say, this takes courage and profound faith. A man by the name of Bill Kreidler once remarked, "Whenever I give workshops, I often go around the room and ask people to give a reason they have for not praying ... I will never forget the woman who said, 'I am afraid of what God will ask me to do.' And I thought, 'You know, that is a darn good reason not to pray.'"

In all our endeavors, we are called to use wisdom and to be guided by God's Spirit. It's no good poking sticks into every hornet's nest we find. But if the Lord calls us to a particular ministry, we need to move forward with faith, no matter what we face. Several years ago, I served on the board of directors for a local pregnancy counseling center. It was a volunteer organization dedicated to providing support to women with unwanted pregnancies. Our goal was to help women find viable alternatives to abortion. Because this approach was considered politically incorrect by many in the college town in which it was located, the center was frequently picketed by students determined to shut it down.

One day, we learned that a group of students was planning to picket the center the next morning. Board members were asked to gather at the center just prior to the picket in order to support staff and volunteers. The night before the picketing was to take place, one of the board members called, explaining that she had been praying about the situation. She suggested that we serve the picketers donuts and coffee. This crazy idea was so outside of my thought process that I decided it might really be from God. The next morning, feeling ridiculous, we braved the bitter cold holding trays of coffee and donuts, which we offered to the bewildered protestors. Meanwhile cameras from a television station in Detroit were rolling, recording the scene. Our surprising gesture made the news that day. It also created an opening for us to talk constructively with those who opposed our work.

Years later, I was surprised to hear that another pregnancy counseling center had done the same thing after hearing about our situation. I'm not sure what the results were, but their action struck me as strange. I knew we had responded to God that day, but I didn't think he had revealed a precise methodology for dealing with dissent. In other words, what might be a Spirit-inspired approach in one situation might not be the best approach in another. The point is to listen to the promptings of the Spirit and respond accordingly.

As men and women called to be like the God we serve, we are to be peacemakers whose vision of what life can be is shaped by the *shalom* God promises. Sharing that *shalom* is not always easy. Sometimes it will be controversial or even dangerous. Learning how to become a "non-anxious presence" at home, at work, and in our community can help us to spread the peace God gives. Ultimately, there are no shortcuts or secrets to peace. Peace is not something mysterious or elusive. The peace we long for, the peace the world so desperately needs, comes as a consequence of our relationship with God. It's a fruit of the Spirit that develops as we try to emulate the Christ we love.

Now that we know the source of our peace—God himself—what are some ways we can connect ourselves to God and experience his peace more deeply? Next we'll look at how the classic Christian practices of reading the Bible, praying, attending church, and celebrating a day of rest can help us find the peace that God promises.

PURSUING PEACE

1. Think of a time when you felt a prompting of the Spirit. Did you follow the prompting? What happened?

2. Describe a time in which you or someone you know was able to comfort or lead by exhibiting a "non-anxious presence." What insights did you gain from this experience?

3. Why might it be wrong to apply a "Holy Spirit prompting" from one situation to another situation?

Part Two

PEACE IN SPIRITUAL PRACTICES

Finally, brothers and sisters, rejoice! Strive for full restoration, encourage one another, be of one mind, live in peace. And the God of love and peace will be with you.

2 Corinthians 13:11

Chapter 5

PEACE IN
SCRIPTURE
AND PRAYER

> *Do not be anxious about anything, but in
> every situation, by prayer and petition, with
> thanksgiving, present your requests to God.
> And the peace of God, which transcends all
> understanding, will guard your hearts and
> your minds in Christ Jesus.*
>
> Philippians 4:6–7

D r. Michael Burry has only one good eye, the result of a sur-
gery he underwent after being diagnosed at the age of two
with a rare form of cancer. Though Burry beat the cancer, he lost his
left eye. After that, whenever Michael tried looking someone in the
eye, the person he was looking at would tend to drift left in his field
of vision. That made him feel off balance, always a bit different.

Though an excellent student with the ability to hyperfocus

on subjects of interest, Burry managed to make it through high school, college, and medical school without forging a single lasting friendship. He attributed his social difficulties to being a one-eyed man in a two-eyed world.

Uncomfortable interacting with others, Burry found the practice of medicine challenging. While working sixteen-hour shifts at a hospital in Nashville, he managed to start an investment blog to explain the rationale for his stock picks to anyone who would listen. It didn't take long for a faithful following to develop. Finally, he decided to leave his medical career behind in order to become an investor. Shortly afterward, Burry opened a hedge fund by the name of Scion Capital. Now he could spend hours holed up alone in his office researching stocks and advising his clients via email. Burry's brilliance was soon yielding astonishing returns. In his first year, when the S&P 500 was down nearly 12 percent, Scion was up by 55 percent.

Then something happened that transformed his view of himself. His young son was diagnosed with a classic case of Asperger's Syndrome, a high-functioning form of autism, and Burry began to realize that he, too, had Asperger's. No wonder he had been content to spend hour after hour alone, digesting financial reports that would have put others to sleep. It explained why he was so good at catching details that other analysts missed.

Burry's ability to obsess over topics that interested him served him particularly well with regard to subprime mortgage bonds. Late in 2004 and early in 2005, he spent months poring over hundreds of tedious reports to discover the ins and outs of how the market worked. The more he read, the more he realized that the subprime mortgage market was a gigantic house of cards waiting to collapse with the slightest adverse wind.

While other investors were gobbling up exotic debt instruments full of subprime mortgages, Burry placed a bet against the market by purchasing credit default swaps, insurance policies that acted as a hedge against default. In a little more than two years his bet would pay off big time. By June 2008, Scion Capital had made a gross gain of 726 percent from its inception in November of 2000. During the comparable period, the S&P 500 had returned a little more than 2 percent.

Michael Burry was the first investor to figure out that the subprime mortgage market was headed for collapse. Soon a handful of other investors drew similar conclusions, uncovering a narrative of greed, complexity, stupidity, and fraud within the marketplace. Knowing the true story of what was happening behind the scenes positioned them to make an enormous amount of money. Though some tried to sound a warning bell, nobody would listen. Instead, they were written off as crazy, cranky, paranoid, and hopelessly out of touch with market developments. Because these investors acted on their beliefs by betting against the market, they made billions at the exact moment trillions of dollars were wiped off the market.

Clearly, what you believe makes an enormous difference in how your future will unfold. You may be a one-eyed man in a two-eyed society, but if your vision is clear and you have the story straight, you will stand when others fall.

Narratives, the stories that make sense of our lives and the world in which we live, are important, particularly when it comes to matters of faith. The story you embrace has immeasurable power to shape your life for good or ill. Though the narrative Burry believed was restricted to the financial markets, it illustrates the power of believing in a story that is true even when everyone else tells you it is false. The stories you embrace as true will take you somewhere, often with profound consequences for your life.

THE NEED FOR STORY

More than developing a sound financial narrative to help guide our investments, all of us need an overarching story to help explain the universe and our place in it. Our need for stories—for narratives that make sense of our lives—seems to be baked into our DNA. Perhaps that is why so many millions belong to one of the world's major religions. Hindus, for instance, believe in thousands of gods as well as in a supreme god named "Brahman." Muslims believe "there is no God but Allah, and Muhammad is his prophet." Buddhists embrace the story of their founder, Siddharta Gauttama, and his quest for an end to suffering. Even atheists embrace a narrative of sorts. According to their gospel, the world was created by chance, and we are alone in the universe without a god to guide us. Therefore, we must rely on reason to create a better world, forsaking outmoded beliefs based on superstition and wishful thinking.

What about Christianity? If you had to pick one Bible verse to sum up the story that is Christianity, you might want to choose John 3:16: "For God so loved the world that he gave his one and only Son, that whoever believes in him shall not perish but have eternal life." That's the big story we believe in, the headline that should animate our daily lives. God walked on earth. God loves us. God will use his great power to save us.

But we are prone to forgetting. In the midst of distressing surprises that threaten to overtake us—a death, an illness, a divorce—we lose sight of the big story God is telling. Doubts creep in and bend the narrative in an altogether different direction. Like a stealth bomber sliding in under the radar, Satan whispers lies that sound all too credible. "God has abandoned me." "He must hate me." "He never answers my prayers." "He never loved me in the first place." "Maybe it's all just a fairy tale." Living smack in the middle of our own stories, we get confused about how God's big story makes sense of our own small story.

Judaism, of course, is based on its own sacred story, one that defines the history of its people. In his novel *The Gates of the Forest*, Elie Wiesel quotes an Hasidic saying that goes like this: "God created human beings because he loves stories." Perhaps the opposite could also be said. "God created stories because he loves human beings." Why should God place so much emphasis on stories? For the simple reason that stories can convey truth on several levels—intellectual, emotional, and spiritual. They impact us in ways that a mere recitation of facts would not. At the risk of putting words into God's mouth, one might quote a character in a Virginia Woolf novel who remarked, "In order to make you understand, to give you my life, I must tell you a story."

THE BIBLE: A GRAND NARRATIVE

God gives us his life and helps us to understand himself through the grand narrative contained in the Bible. Though composed over many centuries, with many characters, subplots, and diversions, the Bible is yet a single story—one that tells us many important things about God, ourselves, and the world we live in. It tells us why God created the world, how it became broken, and what his intentions are for fixing it—and us. Without embracing the story

God is telling, our lives remain disconnected and purposeless. We are here today and gone tomorrow with no particular meaning to our life.

In his book *Knowing God*, J. I. Packer underscores the importance of knowing about God: "As it would be cruel to an Amazonian tribesman to fly him to London, put him down without explanation in Trafalgar Square and leave him, as one who knew nothing of English or England, to fend for himself, so we are cruel to ourselves if we try to live in this world without knowing about the God whose world it is and who runs it. The world becomes a strange, mad, painful place, and life in it a disappointing and unpleasant business, for those who do not know about God."

The New Testament carries the biblical story forward, introducing the one Man who makes sense of it all. Though Christians see intimations of Jesus in the Hebrew Scriptures, the New Testament introduces him in the flesh, presenting him as God reaching out to us, becoming one of us, dying and rising from the dead so that our primary relationship can be healed and restored. Because of Jesus we can know the peace of belonging completely to God.

Embracing this story will change your life. It will set your course. It will make all the difference. But how do we embrace it? Of course there is a moment or a whole series of moments in which we assent to this vital truth, in which we tell Christ we are sorry for our sins, asking his forgiveness and inviting him to inhabit our souls. Some people have always believed. Others come to faith more slowly, more painfully, more dramatically. I remember my own conversion—coming to the end of myself and reaching out my hand to God, hoping desperately he would grasp it but not knowing if he even existed. And then came the peace, a sense of well-being that I had never known, an assurance that

I was loved, and held, and protected, like being bathed in goodness, up to my neck in happiness. That was the moment when my yearning was transformed into faith, when the story became mine to believe — and to live.

READING, REMEMBERING, TRUSTING, LIVING

But how to live it? You live it by reading it, first of all, because without reading, how can you remember it, trust it, lean into it? When everything is falling apart around you, you read, remember, and hold onto God's story as though your life depends on it because, of course, it does. But I confess I have not always held onto the story all that well. There is the ever-present temptation to embrace another narrative, to allow another narrator to bend the story in a different direction, telling us that everything depends on us while very little depends on God. Carried along by circumstances, we make the mistake of "catastrophizing" the future — responding to life with frustration and anxiety, as though we believe that every difficulty will in the end overtake and overwhelm us.

This was nearly my condition not long ago. I was struggling with a difficult issue, feeling a sense of despair about a problem to which there seemed no good answer. I had a sense that things were going to end badly, perhaps very badly. The more I thought about it, the worse I felt. In the midst of my anguish, I reached for the Bible, desperate to hear something from God, who had seemed so silent.

I began reading where I had left off the previous day. As I read, the story came alive in a fresh way. It was about events that had occurred more than 2,500 years ago. The Israelites had recently returned from their captivity in Babylon. As I read, a question formed in my mind. The other tribes in the region were doing everything possible to sabotage the work the Israelites were doing as they tried to rebuild the temple in Jerusalem. Why were they so opposed to letting the Israelites worship their God? Suddenly it occurred to me that worship can be dangerous—at least, to God's enemies. The people in that region must have sensed that the Israelites alone would be pushovers but the Israelites with God would be a force too strong to be resisted.

Reading the story helped me remember the power of God, and I saw that this particular story might have application beyond the historical era in which it occurred. Come to think of it, I felt as though I were in the midst of my own personal battle, trying to believe that God would help even though I was tempted to give in to despair. I began to picture my home as a place where God dwells and my heart as God's altar. I worshiped him, thanking him for his love and faithfulness and praising him for his goodness.

As I worshiped, I felt the heaviness lift. A few days later, the intractable problem I had been fretting about took an unexpected turn for the better. Though I hadn't realized it, God was already at work answering my desperate prayers. Though the enemy had wanted me to give up, the Spirit of God helped me find strength by reconnecting with a part of the story of God's people. Reading helped me remember, remembering helped me to trust, and trusting helped me to live in peace.

Peace through Prayer and Bible Reading

Would you be surprised if I told you that the most practical thing you can do to increase your sense of peace is to pray and read the Bible? Part One laid the groundwork for peace. We find the peace God promises when we realize the Father is the only source of peace, his Son gives us access to that peace, and his Spirit enables and empowers that peace. In other words, peace comes from embracing a relationship with all three persons of our triune God. But if that seems esoteric, just remember that the most important path to peace consists of being united to Christ in a vital way. One of the easiest but most overlooked ways of nourishing that relationship is through daily prayer and Bible reading. Why? Because prayer and Bible reading is simply a way of communicating with God, of talking and listening to him.

Most of my own devotional times are ineloquent and uncomplicated. I usually begin by reading through a portion of Scripture, trying to be sensitive to ways in which God may want to speak to me. That primes the pump, putting my mind and heart in the right disposition for prayer.

Reading Scripture is a little like immersing yourself in the language, history, and culture of a foreign country. The more time you spend in that land, becoming familiar with its values, its language, and its stories, the better you understand it. Reading the Bible is like entering a spiritual country. At first it's confusing. You can't keep track of all the kings and kingdoms, the ritual laws, the perplexing customs, the timeline of biblical history. But the more you persist, the more you begin to experience God revealing himself. Its stories become your stories, its values your values. Gradually, you and God come to share a common language and a common history. You find that you can recognize his voice more easily.

Becoming conversant with the Bible so that God can speak to you through its pages takes time and effort. It requires a decision to read Scripture regularly, whether or not you feel like it. Imagine a restaurant whose chefs cook only when the inspiration strikes. If the chefs feel inspired on Monday but not on Tuesday, tough luck for anyone who shows up for a meal on Tuesday. The restaurant would soon go out of business, because most of the time there wouldn't be enough to eat. It's the same with Bible reading. If you only read the Bible when you feel like it, you will lose the steady spiritual nourishment God wants to provide. Scripture is meant to be our bread and butter, building us up by drawing us closer to God and sustaining our communication with him.

So I begin my prayers by reading a portion of the Bible, listening carefully to what God might be saying to me. Then I speak to him, thanking and praising him. Sometimes I pray the Scriptures back to him, using the words of a psalm to proclaim his goodness.

> *Praise the* LORD.
> *Praise the* LORD, *my soul.*
> *I will praise the* LORD *all my life;*
> *   I will sing praise to my God as long as I live.*
> *Do not put your trust in princes,*
> *   in human beings, who cannot save.*
> *When their spirit departs, they return to the ground;*
> *   on that very day their plans come to nothing.*
> *Blessed are those whose help is the God of Jacob,*
> *   whose hope is in the* LORD *their God.*
> *He is the Maker of heaven and earth,*
> *   the sea, and everything in them—*
> *   he remains faithful forever.*
> *He upholds the cause of the oppressed*
> *   and gives food to the hungry.*

The LORD sets prisoners free,
  the LORD gives sight to the blind,
the LORD lifts up those who are bowed down,
  the LORD loves the righteous.
The LORD watches over the foreigner
  and sustains the fatherless and the widow,
  but he frustrates the ways of the wicked.
The LORD reigns forever,
  your God, O Zion for all generations.
Praise the LORD. (Psalm 146)

Or I may simply enumerate all the ways I have experienced God's faithfulness.

If I sense any sin in my life, I simply repent and ask for forgiveness. Sometimes I take a few moments to recall the events of the last twenty-four hours in order to examine my heart. It helps to look carefully at times when I felt upset, probing to discover what was at the root of my emotional response. Did I sin or were other dynamics at work? Examining these in God's presence, asking the help of his Spirit, will help me sort things out with greater wisdom and peace. Again the psalms are great for putting words to our sorrow.

Have mercy on me, O God,
  according to your unfailing love;
according to your great compassion
  blot out my transgressions.
Wash away all my iniquity
  and cleanse me from my sin.
For I know my transgressions,

and my sin is always before me.
Against you, you only, have I sinned
   and done what is evil in your sight;
so you are right in your verdict
   and justified when you judge.
Surely I was sinful at birth,
   sinful from the time my mother conceived me.
Yet you desired faithfulness even in the womb;
   you taught me wisdom in that secret place.
Cleanse me with hyssop, and I will be clean;
   wash me, and I will be whiter than snow.
Let me hear joy and gladness;
   let the bones you have crushed rejoice.
Hide your face from my sins
   and blot out all my iniquity.
Create in me a pure heart, O God,
   and renew a steadfast spirit within me.
Do not cast me from your presence
   or take your Holy Spirit from me.
Restore to me the joy of your salvation
   and grant me a willing spirit, to sustain me.
Then I will teach transgressors your ways,
   so that sinners will turn back to you.
   (Psalm 51:1–13)

After that I simply lay out my needs and the needs of others in intercessory prayer. At times I pray without words, simply holding a person in God's presence, believing he knows what they need. If you want to experience more of God's peace, take Paul's counsel to heart: "Do not be anxious about anything, but in every situation, by prayer and petition, with thanksgiving, present your requests to God. And the peace of God, which transcends all understanding, will guard your hearts and your minds in Christ Jesus" (Philippians 4:6–7).

Praying, I have learned, is a lot like eating. Skipping a meal or two makes me ravenous. Likewise, skipping prayer causes my faith to wither, making me feel anxious and empty. Fortunately, regaining the habit of regular prayer restores my sense that God is with me. Even fifteen or twenty minutes given to God in this way can produce a life of much greater peace.

OUR STORY TOO

Author Lois Tverberg tells of an experience she had while traveling in Israel. Visiting a class of Orthodox Jewish boys one day, she was surprised to hear one of them describe the Scripture passage they had just been reading like this: "We're reading the story of how God brought us out of Egypt and saved us from the Egyptians." Lois couldn't help but notice that the boy had used the pronoun "us" rather than "them," making it sound as though he and his classmates had just crossed the Red Sea along with Moses and the Israelites. Clearly, these students were reading the Bible as though it were their own story. That's how we should read it, because it is our story too.

No matter how much Scripture we read, no matter how much we pray, it is not always easy to see how our own story at any given moment fits into the larger story that God has already told us. But as we will see, when we attend church and live our lives in Christian community, other believers often can see what we cannot, believe when we cannot, act when we cannot. Through the church God works redemption into our lives while also using us to do his work in others.

PURSUING PEACE

1. How does the grand story told in the Bible help you make sense of your life? How does that knowledge bring you peace?
2. If finding peace requires reading, remembering, trusting, and living Bible truths, which step of that process are you missing?
3. How does regular Bible reading and prayer help us to find peace?

Chapter 6

PEACE IN CHRISTIAN COMMUNITY

*Let the peace of Christ rule in your hearts,
since as members of one body you were called
to peace. And be thankful.*

Colossians 3:15

When I arrived in China to adopt my first child, I was surprised to see how many of the babies who were being adopted suffered from positional plagiocephaly. That's a fancy term for flattening of the head. Adoption workers explained that it happens when children spend most of the time lying in their cribs on their backs. Due to the lack of caregivers, most of the babies had little stimulation and were months behind in their development. Some children who were nearly a year old were unable to sit, stand, or even hold up their heads.

Though my nine-month-old daughter didn't suffer from this condition, I remember how puzzled I was when she responded with complete indifference to all the wonderful toys I had brought from America. She wasn't interested in the colorful rattles, the textured teethers, or even the soft little ball so perfect for baby hands to squeeze. It didn't take long for me to realize that she had never been exposed to toys. Everything was new to her, and she didn't know how to respond.

Two years later, when I adopted my youngest, I was invited to tour her orphanage. In one room toddlers were lined up in two rows, eight to a row. Each was sitting in a brand new baby walker. But the children weren't going anywhere. Their little legs merely dangled from their walkers because they weren't strong enough to propel them. One child at the end of the line kept reaching out her hands and yelling. It was Chinese baby talk, but everyone in the room knew exactly what she was saying. "Somebody, anybody, please pick me up and take me home with you!"

Soon after Eastern Europe began opening up to Westerners, a young Romanian orphan named Tara shocked relief workers. Her little skin-and-bones body tottered unsteadily on twig-like legs. She was so small that she looked like a three-year-old rather than a seven-year-old. Like the other children in the orphanage, Tara had spent most of her life in her crib. And like them her growth had been severely stunted. Determined to help, the relief workers began with the obvious. They made sure the children ate well. Then they added a surprising element to their regimen. Each child began receiving regular massages. At first, Tara and the others winced, finding touch a painful thing to bear. But over time they began growing. After several months, Tara was strong enough to run across the room without falling.

Stories like these underline our basic human need for relationships. We are hardwired for connection. Lacking it, our physical, mental, emotional, and spiritual health can become stunted.

Have you ever looked at a connect-the-dot picture before any lines have been drawn between the dots? At first it looks like just a bunch of dots on a page. But once you start filling in the lines, a picture magically appears. Miss one or two of the dots, however, and the picture fails to materialize. It's the same way with peace. You can be doing a lot of things right but still miss out on the peace God promises if you fail to connect all of the dots. One of these is what I call the peace of belonging.

IN SEARCH OF COMMUNITY

Years ago I had the chance to forsake my Midwestern roots for a move to sunny Arizona. Happy to escape the impenetrable clouds of a Michigan winter, I was delighted to wake up every day to brilliant blue skies. There was only one problem. There was almost no sense of community in my neighborhood. The look-alike stucco houses with red-tiled roofs, attached garages, and concrete-fenced backyards made for complete privacy. Most people simply drove into their garages, shut the door behind them, and entered their own private world, where they stayed until it was time to get in their cars and go somewhere. The wide open spaces of neighborhoods where children were free to roam and neighbors interacted were nowhere evident. The design of my neighborhood spoke volumes about our culture's overemphasis on privacy and individualism, values that can work against our sense of belonging and rootedness.

Eventually I made the move back to Michigan, to a neighborhood of tree-lined streets and older homes, to a place that lays claims to the oldest continuous Fourth of July parade in the state. Every year people line the streets to watch the Hollyhock Parade, complete with a neighborhood band, politicians throwing candy, homemade floats, and children riding bikes decorated in red, white, and blue. Easter egg hunts and frequent get-togethers in neighbors' homes make it seem like you've been transported back into the 1950s. This is a place where people feel a sense of belonging. That's why they move here.

Without a sense of belonging, we become isolated and lonely, attempting to live without a network of close friends and family. No wonder we experience life as stressful and find it difficult to sense God's peace.

When bicycles became the rage in the early part of the twentieth century, at least one group of people opted out. The Amish banned them because they were afraid that bicycles would carry them too far from home. As quaint as that sounds, they were at least thinking about the dynamics of community life. What would help and what would hinder community—that was their primary concern. When scooters came along, similar concerns were voiced. So the Amish bishops called a meeting to decide whether to ban them. But the ban was voted down. Perhaps the vote had something to do with the fact that all the bishops had arrived at the meeting on scooters!

The Amish are experts on community. On average, an Amish grandma has as many as fifty grandchildren while the average Amish person has more than seventy-five first cousins. Furthermore, studies have shown that the Old Order Amish suffer from major depression at rates that vary from one-fifth to one-tenth of the general population in the US. Despite a diet filled with gravy, fried foods, dumplings, and sugar-filled sweets like whoopee pie, the Amish also have much lower rates of heart disease than do average Americans. Some of these findings may be linked to their lifestyle, which is built on manual labor. But perhaps the good health of the Amish can also be attributed to the fact that they live in close-knit communities. If healing and health are aspects of biblical *shalom*, it would seem that the Amish are onto something.

Research shows that the more social relationships you have, the longer you are likely to live. People with the fewest relationships are more than twice as likely to die as those with the most social connections. Likewise people with spouses have longer life expectancies than those who don't. The downside, however, is that when they lose their spouse, their risk of dying increases.

LIVING FAITH TOGETHER

Beyond our basic need for community, we have a critical need to belong to a spiritual community, to become part of a group of people who are committed to living out their faith together. Gilbert Bilezikian, professor emeritus of biblical studies at Wheaton College, points out that our need for community stems from the fact that God himself is a community. As some have said, the Father is the Lover, the Son is the Beloved, and the Spirit is the Love between them. No wonder God creates not just individuals but community.

But we are not living in God's perfect world. Sin has fractured it, breaking our relationship with God, with others, and even with ourselves. Bilezikian points out that the cross of Christ is the only thing capable of restoring the kind of community God intends for us. "The very shape of the cross," he says, "suggests the two main transactions that were effected through it. The upright post stands for the restoration of our community with God. But the vertical trunk itself does not make a cross; it also requires a cross-bar. The arms of Jesus were stretched on that horizontal beam, and his servant hands nailed to it. His extended arms reach out from the crossbar to all who want reconciliation with God in order that we may also be reconciled to one another, forming one body in his embrace of love."

"Perfect community," Bilezikian goes on to say, "is to be found at the intersection of the two segments of the cross, where those who are reconciled with God are reconciled together — where we love God with all we have and we love our neighbor as ourselves." Take out the cross beam and the cross collapses.

So we were made for belonging — belonging to God and belonging to others who have, like us, discovered the saving power of the cross. By his death and resurrection, Jesus restores *shalom*, overcoming the power of sin to rob us of all that God intends to give us. Author Kelly Kapec points out that the Heidelberg Catechism poses a question we all need to ask ourselves: *What is your only comfort in life and in death?* The answer? *That I belong — body and soul, in life and in death — not to myself but to my faithful Savior, Jesus Christ.*

But as Kapec points out, those of us in the affluent West may find the notion of belonging to God a bit insulting. We dislike the thought of being anyone's slave or anyone's servant. When life is challenging, it's nice to think that we are standing next to a big, big God. But what about the times when God demands something of us, when he asks us to make our surrender real through our obedience?

Many of us define ourselves by what we possess — a great job, a trophy wife (or husband), a big house, successful children.

These things tell others who we are—or so we think. But Kapec points out that, "Our sense of self can become so wrapped up with the idea of self-ownership that the thought of belonging to somebody else—including God—looks like a threat and not a hope. Fearing to give, we grasp ever more tightly ... and cling to the impression that we own our bodies, our money, our ideas, our time, our property, and everything else we can manage to slap our name tag on."

We are like those comical seagulls in the movie *Finding Nemo*, forever squawking, "Mine, Mine, Mine, Mine."

Giving ourselves away, forsaking our right to self-determination, can feel terrifying. But it would be tragic to let that fear rule our destiny, keeping us from experiencing the deepest kind of happiness there is. For only union with God can satisfy the hunger he has placed within us. As Psalm 100:3 proclaims, "Know that the LORD is God. It is he who made us, and we are his." And as Paul says, "whether we live or die, we belong to the Lord" (Romans 14:8). To belong to Christ and to his people brings a sense of belonging, a sureness that we who were once lost have at last been found. We find peace because we are no longer orphans. We belong to God's family even though his family on earth still has many problems.

INDIVIDUALS VERSUS GOD'S PEOPLE

If you were to take time to read through the entire Bible, you would discover that it is not primarily a book about how God relates to individuals but about how he relates to his people. Even his dealings with Old Testament figures like Abraham, Moses, Deborah, and David always have a communal dimension to them because these were the leaders through whom God was working to bless, chasten, and guide his people.

By contrast, our own religious bestseller lists are populated with books that contradict this biblical tendency. Instead, they promote individual spiritual fulfillment to the exclusion of all else. But pick up any Bible promise book, examine the context in which each of the promises were given, and ninety-nine times out of a hundred you will discover that God's promises were given to his people as a whole, not to individuals. If you want to live a life of blessing and fulfillment—of biblical *shalom*—you cannot do so on your own but only within the context of Christian community.

Community is meant to be a place where we are healed and strengthened, where we can experience mercy and forgiveness as we encounter others who, like us, desire to grow in Christlikeness. Community is also a place to discover our gifts so that we can become useful for God's purposes. Together with others, we can make a difference in the world. Without community, it is easy to be swept along by the desires that define most people. The lure of money, sex, and power and their affiliated evils can be difficult to withstand. Without brothers and sisters to remind us of what we are living for, we lose sight of the kingdom God is building, forgetting that together we are called to do his work.

For the last several years, I've had the pleasure of meeting weekly with a small group of Christian friends who are determined to support each other in their life with Christ. This is a place where I can talk about my fears and struggles without fear of rejection. When I am weak, I am bolstered by their strength. To paraphrase the words of Dietrich Bonhoeffer, there are times when the Christ in my heart is weaker than the word in my sisters' hearts. My heart is uncertain while theirs are sure. Conversely, there are times when my strength helps them.

One of our shared commitments involves prayer. Often the lists are long—a neighbor who is dying, a friend who's desperate for work, a person who is deeply troubled. After we make our lists, we take them home and pray through them during the course of the week. Last week, we decided to do something different. Each woman shared her requests and then everyone in the group prayed for her. As each person prayed, you could sense God speaking. If one of us had been missing, something important would have been missing from our prayer. It seemed as though the Holy Spirit was using our different voices to express God's heart more fully to that person.

One of the many things community teaches us, Parker Palmer observes, is that "our grip on truth is fragile and incomplete, that we need many ears to hear the fullness of God's word for our lives."

A story is told about a village church built by a wealthy man. Touring the completed building, the townspeople expressed their pleasure in their new church. The stained glass, the stonework, the wood—all of it was beautifully crafted. Yet something vital was missing. When someone asked why the church had no lighting, the man who built it instructed each family, handing them a lamp: "Bring this lamp whenever you come to church and hang it on the end of the pew. When you are there, the church will be filled with light. When you are absent, the light will grow dimmer." Like this village church, our own churches are meant to be places where the light of Christ can shine, where community can thrive, and where people of every race, tribe, and tongue can know the peace that comes from belonging to God and to his people.

The New Testament tells us that united to Christ we are members of his body. Together we are his eyes, his ears, his hands, his voice. People see Christ in us or they do not. Together we make him visible and audible, a tangible presence in a world that is dying to know him.

A STUMBLING, BUMBLING CHURCH

Perhaps you have already tried church and found it nothing like the kind of community I have been describing. Your church might have felt small-minded, dysfunctional, or dull. Recently a bestselling author whose conversion to Christianity caused a stir a few years ago made this statement on her Facebook page: "Today I quit being a Christian. I'm out." Anne Rice was fed up with some of the public positions taken by her church. Later she tried to explain that she still considered herself a follower of Christ but that she wanted nothing to do with the institutional church, which she saw as un-Christlike and unloving.

It's true that the church throughout its history has often stumbled, sometimes terribly. But that is not the whole story. Over its long history, the church has also lifted up the poor and brought healing to the sick and redemption to the lost. Where there has been great darkness, it has often brought great light. Whether Rice is offering a needed corrective to the church or simply letting her political convictions trump all is open to question. But to act as though one can still be a Christian while "quitting Christianity" seems disingenuous. Like it or not, the church is comprised of imperfect human beings. We are not yet who Jesus calls us to be. That is as true of the person who rejects the church as it is of the person who embraces it. That's why God invented forgiveness. That's why he thinks mercy is such a good idea.

In his classic book *Life Together*, Dietrich Bonhoeffer pointed out that we are called to pray for each other. When you pray for someone, he said, you can no longer condemn them no matter how much you dislike them. Why? Because Christ is at work as you pray, transforming an intolerable person into someone for whom he has died. Prayer for others helps us to see the face of a forgiven sinner—and we are all forgiven sinners. Perhaps you have been badly hurt by someone at church. Maybe you have been offended by Christians who seem more concerned about political correctness than the gospel. Or you may have encountered people who are intolerant of anyone who thinks differently than they do.

No matter who in the church is offending you, try praying for them. As Bonhoeffer said, "Even when sin and misunderstanding burden the communal life, is not the sinning brother still a brother, with whom I, too, stand under the Word of Christ? Will not his sin be a constant occasion for me to give thanks that both of us may live in the forgiving love of God in Jesus Christ? Thus the very hour of disillusionment with my brother becomes incomparably salutary, because it so thoroughly teaches me that neither of us can ever live by our own words and deeds, but only by that one Word and Deed which really binds us together—the forgiveness of sins in Jesus Christ." Bonhoeffer went on to say that the Christian "must bear the burden of a brother. He must suffer and endure the brother. It is only when he is a burden that another person is really a brother."

CONFESSING OUR SINS

When we truly belong to others, we begin to feel secure enough to be who we are. At peace with ourselves, we can enjoy life more. For instance, I sometimes do crazy, silly things around my children that I would never think of doing in a public setting. And they do the same around me. Also, when you feel you belong, you can begin to be more honest about your failings. You no longer need to pretend you are better than you are. James tells us we are to confess our sins to one another. But how many of us dare to do so? You may object, saying there's no need to confess your sins to another human being when you have already confessed them to God. But perhaps there is something else that's making confession difficult. Most of us fear rejection and humiliation. We think people will despise us if they know the worst about us.

I'm not suggesting that you confess your sins to everyone. But if you confide in one or two mature Christians who have grasped the gospel and their own desperate need for grace, you needn't fear. You can start with something small and see how the person responds. It takes time to build trust. Then, as the relationship develops, you can disclose more of your struggles. When you confess to a person who is mature in Christ, you will have little to fear and everything to gain.

Have you ever received a prescription drug and then been surprised by all the warnings that come with it? After you've read the prescription information sheet, you may wonder whether you should even take it. If sin came in a package with prescription information attached, this would be the notice printed in bold red type: WARNING—CLINICAL TRIALS HAVE SHOWN THAT SIN CREATES A PROFOUND SENSE OF ISOLATION. IF TAKEN REGULARLY IT WILL LEAD TO SEVERE DEBILITATION AND DEATH.

Sin comes with plenty of strings attached. One of these is its ability to isolate us. We feel separated from God's love, guilty and condemned. Have you ever watched a nature video in which a wolf or cougar or some other predatory animal begins tracking a herd? The predator looks for animals on the outskirts of the herd. The animal that's easiest to take down is the one that has gotten separated from the group. They're the ones that get eaten. Similarly, sin separates us from other believers in the hope of destroying us.

Confession is a protection. It's a medicine we'd rather not take, but it's one that robs the devil, who seeks to devour us, of his power. Instead of feeling condemned, confession allows us to experience God's love and mercy through our sisters and brothers. Another human being knows the worst about us and still loves us. That person manifests Christ's love to us.

Again, Bonhoeffer had remarkable insight into how confession can break through our isolation. Why is it, he asked, that we find it easier to confess our sins to a holy God rather than to another human being? Remember that sin is God's implacable enemy. God hates it because he knows that sin breaks *shalom*. It distorts the world he has made, keeping us from experiencing the peace he promises. Perhaps, Bonhoeffer wrote, we have been deceiving ourselves about confessing to God and receiving his forgiveness. Maybe that's why we keep breaking his commandments, committing the same old sins over and over. Perhaps that's why our faith is feeble. Maybe we have only been "confessing our sins to ourselves and also granting ourselves absolution ... Self-forgiveness can never lead to a breach with sin; this can be accomplished only by the judging and pardoning Word of God itself ... Who can give us the certainty that, in the confession and the forgiveness of our sins, we are not dealing with ourselves but with the living God? God gives us this certainty through our brother. Our brother breaks the circle of self-deception."

Bonhoeffer's words may not sit well with everyone, but it is hard to argue with the instruction James gave the early Christians to "confess your sins to each other and pray for each other so that you may be healed. The prayer of a righteous person is powerful and effective" (James 5:16).

Community is meant to be a place for healing and restoration, a place where we can lock arms together as we live out our faith. Proverbs 17:17 tells us that "a friend loves at all times, and a brother is born for a time of adversity." All of us will encounter times of adversity. May each of us find the friends we need to stand firm when life is difficult, and may we become such friends to others.

No church is perfect, but belonging to a community of people who genuinely love Christ is a tremendous gift. If you haven't yet had that experience, don't give up. Keep seeking, asking the Lord to help you find such a place so that you can experience more of the peace he promises.

PURSUING PEACE

1. Why do you think we are hardwired for connection? What might life look like if we weren't?
2. Have you discovered a church that is a vital spiritual community? If so, what are the things that make it feel like community? If not, what can you do either to find a spiritual community or to create one where you are?
3. Have you ever confessed your sins to another person? If so, what was the result? If not, why not?

Chapter 7

PEACE IN
SABBATH REST

*There remains, then, a Sabbath-rest for the
people of God; for anyone who enters God's
rest also rests from their works, just as God
did from his.*

Hebrews 4:9–10

W hen my children were young, I would often prescribe a
timeout whenever they misbehaved. This relatively mild
form of discipline was frequently met with a dramatic show of
resistance—with loud wails and dragging feet. Listening to their
cries of anguish, an outside observer might have concluded that
I had just ordered them to stand in front of a firing squad or
jump into a fiery pit. What, I wondered, was so terrible about
being sent to your room—a place that you had helped to deco-
rate in bright colors and where you had toys and books to amuse
you? If only someone, I thought, would send me to my room. I

would have loved a regular timeout—a moment to rest, gather my thoughts, and be still.

Historian James Truslow Adams tells the story of an explorer cum anthropologist who worked with indigenous people in the upper Amazon. After receiving news that he needed to leave the jungle for a time, the explorer enlisted the help of a local chief and some others for a three-day march out. Their hurried expedition made great progress on days one and two. But when it was time to break camp on the third day, the explorer was surprised to find that the men refused to budge. Questioned about the reason for the delay, the chief explained: "They are waiting. They cannot move farther until their souls have caught up with their bodies."

The story strikes an immediate chord because it captures the sense of "blur" that characterizes much of modern life. No matter what we do or decide, it seems that life inevitably speeds up. Living at warp speed propels us into a way of life in which stress becomes endemic. As we careen through our days, it can feel as though life is slipping out of control, pushing us to move from one activity to another. Interestingly, the man who brought us the story of the Amazonian natives also coined the phrase the "American Dream." Could it be that our cultural dream, despite all the good it has produced, is in danger of running us off track, preventing many of us from enjoying the peace that comes from living in rhythm with nature and our own limitations? Perhaps our dogged pursuit of success has made us like children who think timeouts are designed for one purpose only—to ruin all their fun.

HURRY, HURRY!

John Ortberg tells of asking a wise friend for spiritual direction after he and his family had moved to Chicago several years ago.

That friend was Dallas Willard. Here's how Ortberg recounts their conversation. "I described the pace of life in my current ministry. The church where I serve tends to move at a fast clip. I also told him about our rhythms of family life: we are in the van-driving, soccer-league, piano-lesson, school-orientation-night years. I told him about the present condition of my heart, as best I could discern it. What did I need to do, I asked him, to be spiritually healthy?

"Long pause.

"'You must ruthlessly eliminate hurry from your life,' he said at last.

"Another long pause.

"'Okay, I've written that one down,' I told him, a little impatiently. 'That's a good one. Now what else is there?' I had many things to do, and this was a long-distance call, so I was anxious to cram as many units of spiritual wisdom into the least amount of time possible.

"Another long pause.

"'There is nothing else,' he said. 'You must ruthlessly eliminate hurry from your life.'"

Ortberg concluded that hurry is indeed the enemy of spiritual health, quoting Carl Jung, who remarked that "hurry is not of the devil. It is the devil."

Perhaps that explains why I have never been able to rid myself of one of my least favorite memories. It happened when I was in high school. I was late for class. After stepping out of the car and into the school parking lot, I noticed a sparrow lying injured and broken on the ground. As an animal lover, my first instinct was to pick it up, cradle it in my hands, and make a beeline for help. But I didn't want to be late. So I suppressed the instinct, stepped past the little bird, and hurried into school. I still feel guilty about that choice.

Maybe you have heard of the Good Samaritan Experiment. Researchers at Princeton Seminary instructed several undergraduate seminary students, telling them that their task was to walk over to another building to deliver a talk to a group of freshman students. Half the subjects were instructed to talk about employment opportunities while the rest were told to discuss the parable of the good Samaritan. The seminary students were also told one of three things. First, that they had a few extra minutes to get to the venue for their talk. Second, that they had just enough time. Or third, that they were already late and needed to hurry.

As the students walked over one by one to the building where they were expecting to deliver their talk, they encountered a man slumped against a wall, apparently in need of assistance. The researchers wondered whether the students with the parable of the good Samaritan in mind would be more likely to stop and help. The unsettling truth was that plenty of these students saw the man and just kept walking. The determining factor of who would help and who would not had little to do with what the students were thinking about but everything to do with how hurried they felt.

More than forty years ago, Thomas Merton contended that the pressures of modern life can themselves become a form of violence, saying that "to allow oneself to be carried away by a multitude of conflicting concerns, to surrender to too many demands, to commit oneself to too many projects, to want to help everyone in everything is to succumb to violence ... It kills the root of inner wisdom which makes work fruitful."

Living under this kind of pressure can disrupt our relationships, because pressure seeks an outlet. Too often it erupts as irritability and frustration. Slow-moving drivers, dawdling children, coworkers who need help, a job that takes longer than we anticipated—all can be reduced to obstacles we must fight to overcome. In the midst of the chaos we never step back to think deeply about anything nor do we listen for God's voice. Under such circumstances, it is hard for anyone to flourish.

The poet Judy Brown reminds us that what makes a fire burn is not just the logs but the space that exists between the logs. Without air a fire will soon burn down to nothing. To use another metaphor, borrowed from book design, we all need to build some white space into our lives. Try reading a page jammed full of text. It's not a pleasant experience. Space between the letters and the lines, space to make a margin around the text—this is what makes reading easy on the eye. Similarly, too many good things packed into too few days will destroy our passion for life, leaving us frustrated, tired, and depleted. We need time to rest, to collect ourselves, and to be renewed.

REMEMBER THE SABBATH DAY

Speaking of rest, let's turn for a moment to the Bible and to a people who had rarely known the meaning of rest. Their story can bring insight into our search for peace and God's desire to provide it. Groaning under the heavy hand of their Egyptian overlords, the Israelite slaves cried out, and God answered by sending them a wonder-working, tongue-tied, miracle-producing man named Moses as their leader and deliverer. Three months after leaving Egypt and crossing the Red Sea, hundreds of thousands of these former slaves could be found camped out in the Desert of

Sinai at the foot of a great mountain. Heeding God's call, Moses ascended that mountain and received what have since become known as the Ten Commandments.

You shall not, you shall not, you shall not—Moses listened as God uttered a steady stream of prohibitions. These commands were designed to protect his people's relationship with him, keeping them out of trouble and helping them to prosper. Notably, only two of the Ten Commandments are stated positively. The first of these is this: "Remember the Sabbath day by keeping it holy. Six days you shall labor and do all your work, but the seventh day is a Sabbath to the LORD your God." Though the next sentence is a negative—"On it you shall not do any work"—the primary thrust of the commandment is positive. "For in six days the LORD made the heavens and the earth, the sea, and all that is in them, but he rested on the seventh day. Therefore the LORD blessed the Sabbath day and made it holy" (Exodus 20:8–11).

This commandment tells the people to be like God, to rest, to keep the Sabbath holy. But why did God need to order former slaves to take a day off? If the ancient Israelites had belonged to a labor union, surely one of their first demands would have been for time off.

Anyone who has worked with children institutionalized in orphanages may know the answer to that question. Some of these children exhibit hoarding behaviors when they are first adopted. No amount of abundance will convince them that they will ever have enough to eat, and so they hide food under mattresses and in drawers, wherever they can stash it.

A friend recounted an experience she had as a teacher in a Midwestern high school. The school was hosting a reception for some unusual newcomers, several boys who were among those known as the "Lost Boys of Sudan," young men who had survived a civil war by making epic journeys across dangerous territory to find freedom. Eager to welcome them, the entire school had turned out for the reception. Overwhelmed by the attention, the boys ate little. But when everyone had left, they began stuffing their pockets with all the cookies they could cram into them. Deprivation produces a scarcity mind-set.

In similar fashion the former Israelite slaves must have worried about taking a day off. How could they possibly provide for themselves and their families? It would take a divine command inscribed in stone to get them to treat the seventh day differently than all the rest, trusting that the God who made the heavens and the earth in six days could care for their needs on the seventh. And what would happen when they began to prosper in the Promised Land? Unless they wanted to suffer from high blood pressure, blocked arteries, and coronary heart disease, they would have to limit their working and doing and piling up in a land that was flowing with milk and honey.

Note that in the Bible the number seven is considered a number of perfection. So when Scripture says that God rested on the seventh day after creating the world in six days, we should understand that he did so not because he was worn out from too much creating—as though fashioning all those soaring eagles, sea monsters, and stars had just plain tuckered him out—but to commemorate the fact that everything he had made was perfect and complete. Nothing was broken, bent, or disordered. Everything was exactly as it should be. So God rested, much like a king surveying his realm with perfect satisfaction.

The Sabbath was a taste of the world as it was meant to be, a sign that though creation had become marred and fractured by sin, God had not abandoned what he himself had fashioned. No, he was at work to restore the world that he had made. To the Jewish people, Sabbath was a sign of God's covenant with them (Exodus 31:13–17). To celebrate it was to embrace that covenant. To ignore it was to reject the covenant.

By commanding the Israelites to observe the Sabbath, God was elevating their status from slaves who had spent 430 years in Egypt to free people who no longer needed to work 24/7. Eugene Peterson remarks that the "reason for Sabbath-keeping is that our ancestors in Egypt went for four hundred years without a vacation (Deuteronomy 5:15). Never a day off. The consequence: they were no longer considered persons but slaves. Hands. Work units. Not persons created in the image of God but equipment for making brick. And building pyramids. Humanity was defaced." Their bondage was one more symptom of a universe enthralled to the power of sin.

The Sabbath, however, is subversive of fallen creation and the world as we know it. Why? Because it foreshadows God's triumph over sin and alienation and all the pain that these entail. It is a promise that expresses God's intention to restore the world he has made. By commemorating the Sabbath, the Israelites were expressing their faith in God and in what he was doing. As Mark Buchanan observes, "Sabbath isn't eternity, but it's close. It's a kind of precinct of heaven. A well-kept Sabbath is a dress rehearsal for things above. In finding the rest of God now, we prepare for the fullness of God one day." What a powerful reality. No wonder that one of the first things Hitler did after invading Poland was to forbid the Jews from observing the Sabbath.

The writer to the Hebrews (4:1–11) speaks of the Sabbath as a type or foreshadowing of the rest that belongs to us as God's people. But rather than insisting that believers keep the Sabbath, he simply tells them to "make every effort to enter that rest" (4:11). Though it was the practice of the early Jewish Christians to observe Sabbath, the church fathers of the second and third centuries taught that the Sabbath was not binding on Gentiles. Still, we have much to learn from the Jewish practice of Sabbath keeping.

A SACRED TIME OF PEACE

Rabbi Abraham Joshua Heschel points out that the first holy object in the history of the world was not a mountain or an altar but a day. The Sabbath, he contends, was something entirely new. Other religions celebrated sacredness by designating places or objects as sacred. But "Judaism," he says, "teaches us to be attached to *holiness in time*, to be attached to sacred events, to learn how to consecrate sanctuaries that emerge from the magnificent stream of a year. The Sabbaths," he says, "are our great cathedrals; and our Holy of Holies is a shrine that neither the Romans nor the Germans were able to burn."

Heschel also explains that though God rested, the ancient rabbis spoke as though God had created something new on the seventh day. That something, he says, is *menuha*, the Hebrew word normally rendered as "rest." In the context of the Sabbath passages, rest meant far more than simply taking a day off or engaging in leisurely pursuits. "To the biblical mind," he says, "*menuha* is the same as happiness and stillness, as peace and harmony ... What was created on the seventh day?" he asks. "*Tranquility, serenity, peace* and *repose*." Heschel goes on to say that *menuha* eventually became equated with the life to come. "Six evenings a week we pray: 'Guard our going out and our coming in'; on the Sabbath evening we pray instead: 'Embrace us with a tent of Thy peace.'" The Sabbath is to be like warm shelter, a safe place, a day in which Jewish people can experience God embracing them with his peace.

So Sabbath is much more than leisure. A day at the beach might relax us. A massage and a visit to the spa might delight us. But these do not constitute Sabbath rest. Susannah Heschel, the daughter of Abraham Heschel, comments on how Friday evenings at their home was always the climax of her week as they were for every Jewish family. "Shabbat comes with its own holiness; we enter, not simply a day but an atmosphere." Sabbath is meant to be a foretaste of paradise, a testimony, she says, to God's presence. Her father taught her that just as it was forbidden to kindle a fire on the Sabbath, one must not kindle a fire of righteous indignation. That's why her family refrained from talking about politics, the Holocaust, or the war in Vietnam on the Sabbath, focusing instead on topics that would help create a sense of *menuha*. Her father also taught her that Sabbath was a day for the body as well as the soul and that it was a sin to be sad on that day.

But the peace of Sabbath does not magically materialize. It takes work and preparation. In Jewish homes the preparation often begins early in the week because everything needs to be readied by sundown on Friday when Sabbath begins—a festive meal, a clean house, chores completed, enough food to ensure that no cooking needs to be done for the next twenty-four hours. Somehow this is fitting since Sabbath is intimately connected to the rest of the week, whose days are thought of as a pilgrimage toward the Sabbath.

Sabbath Rules and Regulations

Delightful as Heschel's version of the Sabbath is, it was far different than my first encounter with it, albeit a Christian version. I remember visiting my grandparents one Sunday. To pass the time before dinner, my brother, sister, and I decided to go door-to-door selling magazine subscriptions to raise money for our school. We didn't know that my grandparents lived in the middle of a neighborhood filled with people who took Sunday seriously. After knocking on a couple of doors, we encountered a woman who seemed scandalized by our behavior. Scolding us soundly, she said, "I can't believe you are selling magazines on Sunday!" Then, with a huff, she shut the door in our faces. We had thought we were doing something good by raising funds for our school. Now we felt like scoundrels and cheats though we didn't know why.

Years later when I began working in Christian publishing, I listened in on a conversation in which colleagues took turns describing their own childhood Sundays. Most had grown up in churches that observed strict regulations for how Sundays should and should not be spent. As children they were sometimes puzzled about why they were allowed to do one thing and not another. Many of them concluded that the key variable was "sweat." If an activity made you perspire, it was forbidden. Notably, none of them said anything about experiencing a sense of awe and peace as Susannah Heschel had characterized her own family's observance of the Sabbath.

The Jewish people, of course, are not strangers to the problem of legalism. In their earnest desire to keep God's commandments, they've developed a technique that involves "putting a fence around the law." For instance, instead of merely fasting for twenty-four hours on Yom Kippur, they fast for twenty-five hours, thereby ensuring that they are in compliance with the regulation. But the problem with erecting fences is that life itself can start to feel fenced in by countless rules and regulations.

Believe it or not, one telephone company in Israel offers its ultraorthodox Jewish customers a kosher phone. This useful gadget has been configured to block numbers for phone sex and dating services. It also charges less than two cents a minute compared with the average rate of 9.5 cents. There is only one catch. On the Sabbath, rates are $2.44 per minute! People with these phones are fencing themselves in, preventing themselves from transgressing the command to keep the Sabbath holy.

In his book *The Rest of God*, Mark Buchanan points out that "for a long while legalism was the hound that chased Sabbath, kept it gaunt and haunted." But for most of us that is no longer true, he says. Now the great killer of Sabbath is busyness. Lamenting his own harried schedule, Buchanan says, "I cannot think of a single advantage I've ever gained from being in a hurry. But a thousand broken and missed things, tens of thousands, lie in the wake of all that rushing."

CELEBRATING A DAY OF REST

Perhaps it is good that Christians are not bound to observe the Sabbath as outlined in the Hebrew Scriptures. Choosing the Sabbath freely can enable us to experience it with joy. But how can we find a way to taste the goodness of Sabbath or, better yet, to incorporate it into our lives on a regular basis? Observing the Sabbath, even partially and imperfectly, will require us to make decisions. Can we designate one day a week, perhaps a Saturday or Sunday, or even one day a month for a special Sabbath meal? If that seems too hard, perhaps we can begin by setting aside an afternoon and evening.

Andrea Doering is a professional woman, wife, and mother who decided a few years ago to begin celebrating a day of rest with her family. She remembers what provoked the decision. Looking forward to her vacation, she had been working overtime to make sure everything was done before heading out. But by the time her vacation rolled around, she was so exhausted that she became sick and didn't recover until she returned home. At least one good thing resulted from that wretched vacation—the realization, she says, that rest isn't something we are supposed to save up. We need it every week.

Longing for more balance in her life, she decided that God's best idea for rest could be found by observing the Sabbath. What if she and her family were to set aside one day a week to rest? Noting that her job required her to sell things, it occurred to her that she was reacting either as a consumer or as a seller every day of the week. So that was the first thing to go. No shopping for twenty-four hours. She wouldn't even allow herself a moment to check prices on her favorite website.

Though her children objected, she also decided that there would be no play dates on that day. She felt guilty at first, but she knew how difficult it was for her to rest whenever one of her children went off somewhere. There were always practical arrangements to make, getting them ready, dropping them off, or picking them up.

Other decisions included no family parties on that special day and no chores. She was even careful to put away any visual reminders of work, stashing briefcases and backpacks out of sight. Now she and her family observe their day of rest beginning Friday night and ending Saturday night or starting Saturday morning and ending after Sunday morning worship service.

How does Doering get everything done the rest of the week? She shops for groceries on Sunday afternoon, relegating other shopping trips to weeknights. The unexpected dividend of that arrangement is that weeknight outings are automatically limited to two hours or less because of school and work the next day.

How has her family responded? Her husband is firmly onboard. Though her children aren't always thrilled with the limitations of the day, they appreciate having one day free to sleep in and do whatever they want. Setting aside a definite time for rest, she says, has become for her and her family a declaration of independence. They are no longer slaves to consumerism or to the clock.

Observing a day of rest has also brought some surprising insights. When Doering subtracted the chores, the shopping, and all the other responsibilities that had always defined her life, she felt adrift, uncertain of how she should spend the time. As the mother of young children, it had been so long since she'd had time to herself that she couldn't even remember what she liked to do. So the first order of business was to make a list of everything she could think of that sounded fun and enjoyable for her day of rest. Cycling, kayaking, gardening, and playing games together — even talking on the phone with her sisters — these were all items that had been pushed aside by the daily routine. Now there was time to enjoy them again.

Doering was also surprised to note that most of her conversations with her children involved telling them what to do. "Remember your lunch." "Pick up your clothes." "Get ready for school." Suddenly there was no need for such instructions because there was nothing they *had* to do. For their part, her children were delighted to have a Sabbath rest from being told what to do all the time. Since then, their mother has found ways to focus more of her conversation on things that interest them.

Her desire for balance is what had driven the search for rest in the first place. And even though she and her family are not observing the Sabbath as a Jewish family would, her efforts to carve out a day of rest have resulted in a surprising insight. Having the time to reflect on her life brought with it the realization that God isn't as interested in balance as she is. "Balance," she explains, "says that all things should be equal, but God says that nothing is equal to him." That insight put everything in its proper place. Nothing took precedence over her relationship with God.

Is she ever tempted to revert to life as it used to be now that her children are teenagers? Doering answers with a definite no. It can be challenging to be out of sync with the rest of the world, she admits, but she and her family have experienced too many benefits from their day of rest to return to their old ways.

A JEWISH SABBATH

However you decide to build more rest into your own life, you may find it helpful to look at how the Sabbath is observed in Jewish homes. On Sabbath most people serve the best food they can afford. They also wear their best clothes. Often they invite family, friends, or others in need of special encouragement to join them. A few flowers and a clean house enhance the experience for everyone. As Lois Tverberg has remarked, "In Judaism, the Sabbath is a real joy, a delight, a grand party. It focuses on the good things God *does* want people to enjoy."

Here's an abbreviated version of what happens in an observant Jewish home. Two candles are placed on the table along with
a cup of wine or grape juice and two loaves of *challah* (a braided
bread that can be baked or purchased at a local bakery). The
loaves are covered by a cloth or napkin.

Before the candles are lit, everyone, even young children, give
tzedakah (charity) by placing a few coins in a special *tzedakah*
box. That way everyone at the table can participate in what the
rabbis call *tikkun olam*, a Hebrew phrase meaning the "repair of
the world."

Then the woman of the house lights both candles and wel-
comes the Sabbath by waving her hands over them, closing her
eyes, and praying in Hebrew:

> *Blessed are you, Lord our God, King of the universe,*
> *Who sanctifies us with his commandments,*
> *and commands us to light the lights of Shabbat.*

Everyone then either attends a brief evening service at the
local synagogue or continues the prayer at home. At some point
in the evening, it is customary for the father (sometimes the
mother) to place his hands on his children's heads in order to
pray a special blessing on them.

Next, a blessing called the *Kiddush* is said while a cup of wine
or grape juice is held up:

> *And there was evening and there was morning,*
> *a sixth day.*
> *The heavens and the earth were finished, the whole*
> *host of them.*

And on the seventh day God completed his work that
 he had done
and he rested on the seventh day from all his work
 that he had done.
And God blessed the seventh day, and sanctified it
because in it he had rested from all his work that God
 had created to do.
Blessed are you, Lord, our God, King of the universe
who creates the fruit of the vine (Amen).
Blessed are you, Lord, our God, King of the universe
who sanctifies us with his commandments, and has
 been pleased with us.
You have lovingly and willingly given us your holy
 Shabbat as an inheritance, in memory of creation
because it is the first day of our holy assemblies, in
 memory of the exodus from Egypt
because you have chosen us and made us holy from
 all peoples
and have willingly and lovingly given us your holy
 Shabbat for an inheritance.
Blessed are you, who sanctifies Shabbat (Amen).

The cup of wine or juice is passed around the table and every-one takes a drink.

After that people wash their hands by pouring water from a cup, first over their right hand and then their left. Another prayer is prayed. Then the man of the house removes the napkins covering the loaves of bread, lifts them up, and recites this blessing:

Blessed are you, Lord, our God, King of the universe,
Who brings forth bread from the earth.

With that he tears a piece from the loaf and passes the bread around so that everyone can have some. Then the meal begins. During dinner someone usually offers a commentary on the weekly Torah portion, the Scripture reading for the morning service on Saturday, which everyone has read prior to the Sabbath ceremony. After the meal there are more prayers and singing.

Rabbi Joseph Telushkin points out that when a father, a mother, or both parents bless their children prior to the meal, they often press their lips against their child's forehead and say to a son, "May God make you like Ephraim and Manasseh" (Genesis 48:20), and to a daughter, "May God make you like Sarah, Rebecca, Rachel, and Leah" followed by: "May the Lord bless and protect you! May the Lord deal kindly and graciously with you! May the Lord bestow his favor upon you and grant you peace" (Numbers 6:24–26). Many parents, he says, add a special blessing for each child.

Why does the father pray that God will make his sons like Ephraim and Manasseh? Telushkin quotes Rabbi Shlomo, who says: "It's precisely because Ephraim and Manasseh got along so well that they are mentioned, because most brothers in the Torah (Cain and Abel, Isaac and Ishmael, Jacob and Esau, Joseph and his brothers) didn't." Whenever Telushkin was away from home on the Sabbath, he would telephone to give his children the blessing. Remembering his usual kiss, his six-year-old daughter would hold the phone against her forehead when she heard him reciting the blessing.

Christians often think that worship can only take place in church. But for Jews, the home is the center of worship. The dinner table is considered the family altar and the home a little sanctuary where God can dwell. Squabbling kids and busy schedules may make it hard for you to imagine that your table could ever become an altar. But what if you began thinking of it like that, treating it as a special place and teaching your children to do the same? It must be possible. Otherwise observant Jews would have abandoned the practice long ago.

Christians who want to celebrate the Sabbath may want to adapt the Jewish ceremony for their own use. Resources for Messianic Shabbat liturgies can be found on the Internet. Some Christians may prefer to celebrate on Saturday night until sundown on Sunday, remembering that Sunday is a special day to worship God and celebrate the resurrection. Whatever you decide, Sabbath can be a special time of sensing God's presence, of living and speaking in ways that bring peace to yourself and others. Sabbath is not about adhering to rules and regulations but about celebrating what God has done and is doing. So worship God, eat well, take a walk, soak in a bubble bath, play games, go kayaking, rest, and enjoy!

Sabbath keeping and other spiritual practices can add immeasurably to our sense of peace. There are times when difficulty and strife may threaten to undo us. Yet, even in the most extreme circumstances, God has promised to give us peace of heart and mind.

PURSUING PEACE

1. How would you describe the pace of your life right now: faster than a speeding bullet, slower than a slug, or somewhere in between? What kind of impact — positive or negative — does the pace at which you are living have on your ability to experience rest and peace?

2. Enough space between the letters and lines of a page of text is what makes reading easy on the eye. How could you build more space into your life in order to experience more of God's peace?

3. How does celebrating a Sabbath—a day of rest—help you to experience the peace that God promises?

4. What changes would you have to make in order to be able to set apart one day a week as a day of rest? How might your life change if you could make those changes?

Part Three

PEACE OF HEART
AND MIND

And the peace of God,

which transcends all understanding, will guard

your hearts and your minds in Christ Jesus.

Philippians 4:7

Chapter 8

PEACE IN
THE MIDST
OF SUFFERING

"Though the mountains be shaken and the hills be removed, yet my unfailing love for you will not be shaken nor my covenant of peace be removed," says the LORD, who has compassion on you.

Isaiah 54:10

Barbara Arrowsmith Young knows something about finding peace after a long period of suffering. Severely dyslexic as a child, Barbara had difficulty reading and comprehending what she read. "If I read something forty times or replayed a discussion in my head for hours," she explained, "I would eventually come to understand it." She couldn't fathom why other children had to do only one-tenth of the work she did in order to achieve the same results. Barbara had so much trouble understanding social

119

situations that she sometimes reviewed conversations as many as twenty times before she could make sense of them.

Though no one knew it at the time, she was suffering from a learning disorder that made it difficult for her to understand relationships between symbols, which in turn made it impossible for her to understand math, grammar, or logic. What Barbara did have going for her, however, was an extraordinary memory and enough sheer grit to make it into a graduate program in psychology. Her breakthrough finally came when she was introduced to the work of two researchers—Alexander Luria and Mark Rosenzweig. Luria was a Russian psychoanalyst and neuropsychologist who had succeeded in mapping the brain, discovering which area of the brain was responsible for which function. Rosenzweig was a psychologist who had conducted experiments that demonstrated neuroplasticity, the theory that stimulation can change the brain's structure and functional wiring. In layman's terms, neuroplasticity means that with the right kind of stimulation, your brain can repair and heal itself. Prior to the development of this theory, it was thought that brain injuries were irreversible.

Putting the findings of these two scientists together, Barbara realized that she might be able to heal herself. So she began to design exercises to stimulate specific areas of her brain in order to restore function in each area. Using herself as a guinea pig, she performed these exercises over and over, hours on end, until she experienced a change. As time progressed, she could understand grammar, logic, and math with much greater ease.

By directly targeting the weaknesses in her own brain, Barbara was adopting the opposite approach to the one normally taken with people who have learning disabilities. According to the usual model, a child who has difficulty reading will be given audio books as a way to compensate for his or her weakness. But instead of avoiding her weaknesses in order to play to her strengths, Barbara worked on strengthening her weaknesses, with incredible results. When I met her a year ago, I encountered an intelligent, compassionate, and articulate woman who had no difficulty maintaining a high level of conversation even in the midst of a noisy restaurant. Had I not already known something of her story, I would never have guessed that Barbara Arrowsmith Young had once been labeled "retarded."

In the last thirty-some years, she has dedicated her life to developing one of the most innovative educational programs in the world. Designed for children with learning disorders, the Arrowsmith Program, headquartered in Toronto, is described as "Olympic training for the brain." Her work has tremendous import for helping learning-disabled children.

During our dinner together, Barbara noted that the learning disabilities that had made her life so painful, causing her to feel isolated and depressed as a child, were the very things that had enabled her to help so many others overcome their own disabilities. Her story has great meaning, not only for herself but for the countless children helped by her work. She has made peace with her suffering because it gave her life purpose and meaning.

Parker Palmer talks about how our suffering sometimes can be put into perspective by the passage of time. "In retrospect, I can see in my own life what I could not see at the time—how the job I lost helped me find work I needed to do, how the 'road closed' sign turned me toward terrain I needed to travel, how losses that felt irredeemable forced me to discern meanings I needed to know. On the surface it seemed that life was lessening, but silently and lavishly the seeds of new life were always being sown."

FOCUS ON GOD FIRST

Sometimes the challenges we face are less dramatic, small irritations or worries that can build our minds into something worse. Even with small frustrations it's easy to fall into a habit of "catastrophizing" the future. My mother, for instance, is always misplacing her glasses. As soon as she finds they are not in her purse, she is certain she has lost them forever. What will she do without glasses? It will cost a fortune to buy another pair. She can't drive without glasses. When will she find time to get to the optometrist? A little more searching usually ends with a sigh of relief as she locates the missing glasses. This process takes about a minute and a half. After so many repetitions of this scenario, it would be reasonable for my mother to assume that she has simply misplaced her glasses, not lost them forever. But her mind goes straight to the worst-case scenario. The same can happen on a larger scale whenever we are facing some kind of difficulty.

When one of my children is suffering and I am unable to help her, I am tempted to believe that God will not hear my prayers. When a friend is trying hard month after month to land a job but nothing opens up, I am tempted to believe that her circumstances are too intractable for God to handle. When someone I care about stubbornly heads down a dangerous path, I can be fooled into thinking only I can save him. When a cherished hope fails, I forget that God is faithful and that the future is still good. Placing myself and my problems at the center of the universe, I forget who the real hero of the story is.

Perhaps you do the same thing. It's so easy to forget all the ways God has already helped you if you are focusing on the difficulty you face right now. St. Paul counseled the early Christians in this way, saying, "Whatever is true, whatever is noble, whatever is right, whatever is pure, whatever is lovely, whatever is admirable—if anything is excellent or praiseworthy—think about such things. Whatever you have learned or received or heard from me, or seen in me—put it into practice. And the God of peace will be with you" (Philippians 4:8–9). Paul makes a guarantee. *Do* these things *and* the God of peace will be with you!

Too often I forget Paul's sage advice. Instead I find myself fixated on whatever is threatening, whatever is difficult, whatever is miserable, whatever is bugging me—if anything is broken or bad—I think about such things. Little wonder that at such times the God of peace seems far away. Instead of getting distracted by our difficulties, we need instead to focus on God first and what he has promised to do with our lives.

When Moses sent twelve men to scout out the land of Canaan, only two came back with a positive report. All twelve had seen exactly the same thing, but they returned with completely different interpretations. Joshua and Caleb couldn't wait for Moses to lead the people into a land flowing with milk and honey. Yes, the Canaanites were powerful and their cities were large and well-fortified, but these two men were confident that God would deliver their enemies into their hands. By contrast, the other ten scouts were fixated on the obstacles, describing the inhabitants of Canaan as giants, compared to whom they were mere grasshoppers. According to them, the Israelites would be devoured if they tried to invade this land.

What would you have done in such a situation? I might have listened to the ten "reasonable" men, whose observations seemed to offer a large dose of common sense. After all, those Canaanites were big guys. Their cities did look impregnable. But this apparently reasonable take on the scene was all wrong because these ten men failed to build God into their narrative, doubting that he could deliver on his promise.

All of us have to face many difficulties in our lives. At such times, we cannot afford to entertain peace-destroying thoughts and beliefs that will take our gaze away from Jesus. Exercising our imagination in a negative way will inevitably steal our peace, making us fearful, frustrated, and depressed. What's more, if we develop a pattern of negative thinking, we risk becoming "practical atheists," people who call themselves Christians even though they think and act just like atheists.

Instead of forgetting, we need to remember who God is and what he has already done for us, believing that he knows everything we are going through, everything we are up against.

The other day a reader wrote to tell me about how she clung to God during something tragic that occurred in her life a year earlier. Francoise wrote: "My husband told me he didn't love me any more and refused to work it out. He was done. I didn't know that I could feel so much heart pain. It was so bad that there were times when it felt as if I were having a heart attack. The previous year, I'd recommitted my life to God. Little did I know at the time of my yielding all to him that it would mean rapid and sometimes devastating change. Through the pain and chaos, I refused to doubt. And I told God out loud that I knew he was good and faithful. I chose to believe what I knew of him. The very morning that I left my husband, God told me that he was my husband now. He said he was taking me out of Egypt for the last time, and I would not leave empty handed."

A year later, here's how she characterizes her life: "I have come through the other side with more healing and freedom to love God than I knew would be possible! And I'm confident that the best is yet to come!"

Psychologist Ed Welch wrote a book a few years ago entitled *When People Are Big and God Is Small.* I love the title because it captures the root cause for our lack of peace. We suffer whenever our perspective gets out of whack. Whenever our problems seem big and our God seems small, we lose our peace. Whenever we remember how big God is, how capable and in control he is, once again we can relax and entrust all things — big and small — to his loving care.

CATASTROPHIC SUFFERING

Sometimes, however, the suffering we endure is no small thing. Like Barbara Arrowsmith Young, we might someday be able to look back on our difficulties with gratitude for how God has used them. And like Francoise, sometimes we will be able to look beyond the challenges facing us to the God who is bigger than us. But sometimes no redemptive story will emerge, and sometimes the hurt will be so catastrophic that we will have to put the tragedy into God's hands, again and again.

I lost my sister in a car accident when she was only sixteen. A careless man ran a red light on a foggy October morning, ramming his truck into our car. That was decades ago, and I have yet to discover a redemptive purpose for her death. I cannot make sense of it, but that does not prevent me from entrusting my sister and my grief into God's hands, believing that he is able to bring something good out of something that is not good.

Joni Eareckson Tada has been a quadriplegic for most of her life. She broke her neck in a diving accident when she was only seventeen. Despite, or perhaps because of her hardships, she has developed a vibrant faith. From her wheelchair she tells us:

"The cross is the center of our relationship with Jesus. The cross is where we die. We go there daily. It isn't easy.

"Normally, we will follow Christ anywhere—to a party, as it were, where he changes water into wine, to a sunlit beach where he preaches from a boat. But to the cross? We dig in our heels. The invitation is so frighteningly individual. It's an invitation to go alone.

"Suffering reduces us to nothing and as Søren Kierkegaard noted, 'God creates everything out of nothing. And everything which God is to use, he first reduces to nothing.' To be reduced to nothing is to be dragged to the foot of the cross. It's a severe mercy.

"When suffering forces us to our knees at the foot of Calvary, we die to self. We cannot kneel there for long without releasing our pride and anger, unclasping our dreams and desires ... In exchange, God imparts power and implants new and lasting hope."

As Joni found, catastrophic suffering imposes a terrible burden on us, a cross as cruel and painful as the one Jesus endured. Yet even in the midst of our struggles, God will not forsake us. He will give us the strength to endure and new hope based in him.

PEACE AT THE TIME OF DEATH

For most of us, death is the place where we most need God's peace. A few years ago, when my father lay dying, I prayed to be present at his bedside at the moment of his death. God graciously answered that prayer, enabling me to enter his hospital room just sixty seconds before he passed, enough time to whisper the Lord's

Prayer in his ear. My mother and brothers were present as well. I will never forget the moment of his death because it was one of the most peaceful moments of my life. But as anyone who has experienced death close up knows, it can often be ugly and jarring. My father had been sick for many months. He looked gaunt and drawn from the ravages of his long struggle. Ordinarily such a scene would inspire revulsion rather than peace. But God was so present in that room that I didn't want to leave. His peace was palpable.

Todd Smith is a vocalist for the band Selah. He and his wife, Angie, are parents to three young daughters and an infant who lived only briefly. Her name was Audrey Caroline. Because of her belief in the sanctity of human life, Angie was determined to carry her daughter to term when a twenty-week ultrasound revealed that the baby was suffering from a lethal condition. The weeks that followed were filled with prayer. But when the baby was delivered by cesarean section, Angie and Todd had only two-and-a-half hours with their daughter before she passed away.

In a letter to Audrey that Angie later wrote, she said, "I didn't feel like I lost a baby; I felt like I said goodbye to someone I had always known."

Neither Todd nor Angie understand why their daughter's life had to be so brief. They still grieve. But as Todd explains, "There are a lot of things that are just unanswered. And it is just as simple and as hard as trusting Him because I don't have another option."

One of the songs on Selah's album *You Deliver Me* speaks about God's ability to redeem even the most broken aspects of our lives. Take whatever in your life is shattered, it says, and lay it down before the Lord. In his good time it will be restored. Or as

Paul said, "For I am convinced that neither death nor life, neither angels nor demons, neither the present nor the future, nor any powers, neither height nor depth, nor anything else in all creation, will be able to separate us from the love of God that is in Christ Jesus our Lord" (Romans 8:38–39).

PURSUING PEACE

1. How has the passage of time given you perspective on a time of suffering in your life?
2. Think of something small that is bothering you right now. How can you focus on God when you suffer from minor irritations?
3. How can major catastrophes grow our faith?
4. How does the promise of God's presence help you face death?

Chapter 9

HEALING
FROM HURTFUL
MEMORIES

Nevertheless, I will bring health and healing
... I will heal my people and will let them
enjoy abundant peace and security.

Jeremiah 33:6

Several years ago, during the first Intifada, when hostilities between Palestinian Arabs and Israelis were even worse than they presently are, I traveled to Israel along with a small group of publishing professionals. We had been invited to examine this troubled region of the world by meeting with groups and individuals on various sides of the complex problems that divide the region. We met with Israeli politicians, Palestinian mullahs, Jewish settlers in the Gaza Strip, and members of the Palestinian parliament in exile in Jordan. We even "got stoned in the West Bank," to echo the slogans printed on T-shirts hawked in Jerusalem's market stalls. A cadre of young boys had peppered our bus with rocks as we drove by one day.

At the end of the tour, when the rest of the group returned home, I stayed on in Jerusalem for a few days to celebrate Easter in this most fractious of cities. But Holy Week celebrations were marred by a riot in the Old City of Jerusalem, complete with tear gas. The next day I saw the Greek Orthodox Patriarch lead a procession through the winding streets of the Old City, his face lacerated and bruised from the previous day's rioting.

If I had any hope of peace when I first stepped foot in Israel, it had vanished by the time I left. I realized that my American approach to problem solving didn't have much traction in a land where people's historical memories stretch back for centuries, recalling insults and wrongs committed not just decades ago but hundreds of years previously.

I remember meeting with a group of Palestinian Christians who lived in Beit Sahour, a small town that lays claim to the field where angels announced Christ's birth to shepherds watching their flocks at night. When someone in our group suggested to these Christians that part of the solution to Israel's problems might involve relocating people to other areas of this small country, they became indignant, assuring us they would never move even a mile to Bethlehem because that would mean leaving behind a village that had been home to their family for hundreds of years. Their family history, even the memory of past grievances, had developed in this village, shaping their identity so strongly that they could not conceive of leaving it behind.

That experience made me wonder about the ability of entrenched memories, both personal and communal, to poison our search for peace. How should we deal with difficult memories that have become part of our personal history? Should we simply find a way to forget how others have treated us, or could the memory itself be dealt with in a way that could bring us to a place of deeper peace?

REMEMBERING RIGHTLY

Miroslav Volf is a professor of systematic theology at Yale Divinity School. But in the fall of 1983 he was a soldier, drafted into military service in a communist country. Leaving behind his wife, he spent a year on a military base in what was then the Socialist Federal Republic of Yugoslavia. From the moment he stepped on base, Volf felt himself in danger.

The first surprise was his appointment as administrative assistant to the captain in charge of the base. Though he didn't know it, his assignment made it easy for his superiors to keep a close eye on him since the office had been fitted with listening devices. Volf had come under immediate suspicion for three reasons: his father had been a pastor suspected of sedition in the aftermath of World War II; he was a Christian theologian who had studied in the West; and his wife was an American citizen.

One day the captain summoned Volf to his office. There on his superior's desk lay a file, a foot thick, detailing many of his conversations with other soldiers. No wonder so many of them had been asking his views on religion, politics, and the military. The entire base had been spying on him. Volf, the captain stated, was certainly a traitor. Unless he confessed on the spot, he would be imprisoned as a spy. Despite his innocence, Volf felt helpless, knowing that nothing he said would convince the captain otherwise.

Week after week he was interrogated, verbally abused, and threatened. The accusations and threats kept piling up. Finally and without any explanation, the interrogations stopped.

Though Volf calls his mistreatment "mid-level abuse," mild compared to what others have endured, he admits that the effects lingered long after his stint in the military ended. "It was," he said, "as though Captain G. had moved into the very household of my mind, ensconced himself right in the middle of its living room, and I had to live with him.

"I *wanted* him to get out of my mind on the spot and without a trace. But there was no way to keep him away, no way to forget him. He stayed in that living room and interrogated me again and again."

Though Volf was outraged by how he had been treated, he was determined to find a redemptive way of dealing with the abuse he had suffered. Unwilling to grant evil the final victory, letting it shape him into a bitter, vengeful man, he realized that the key lay in *how* he would remember what had happened. He could store up the memory in a bitter, vindictive way, doing damage to his soul in the process; he could absorb it in a masochistic way, forever identifying himself as a victim and thereby giving continued power to his oppressor; or he could try to repress it and simply forget about it. Knowing that none of these options would bring peace or enable him to love his enemy, he searched for another way, one that involved both telling the truth and extending grace without excusing the behavior of his interrogator. What he learned in his quest is told in his book *The End of Memory: Remembering Rightly in a Violent World*, a book that offers great insight into our struggle to find peace despite the memory of wrongs suffered. In the pages that follow we will explore a few of his central insights.

PUTTING BROKEN PIECES TOGETHER

None of us can escape the harm that comes from living in a world ravaged by sin. Often our suffering is caused not by strangers but by those closest to us—a father who rejects his child, a wife who deceives her husband, a teacher who abuses his students, a coworker who sabotages her colleagues. Such offenses can be traumatic. How can we deal with the memory of our hurts in a way that breaks the cycle of pain and opens the door to a greater sense of God's peace?

In his book *The Rest of God*, Mark Buchanan explains that "to remember is, literally, to put broken pieces back together, to *re*-member. It is to create an original wholeness out of what has become scattered fragments." This definition dovetails with the meaning of the word *shalom*, which can be defined as wholeness. So to remember rightly means to restore someone or something to a state of wholeness. Remembering wrongly, by contrast, guarantees that nothing will be put back together right. The original wound will continue to fester. The fracture may heal but it will heal crookedly.

Consider a man who has just lost his job. He's sure that coworkers have been bad-mouthing him, spreading rumors to get him fired. Unfortunately their ploy seems to have worked. Unable to find another job, the man nurses his bitterness, cursing his former coworkers for the way they have slandered him. During the few interviews he does get, he can't help complaining about how badly he was mistreated at his last job. As time passes, the man becomes more frustrated and angry, bent on revenge.

Now here's how the story might have played out had this same man been able to remember rightly. He knows his coworkers have slandered him and that this may have cost him his job. Resisting the urge for revenge, he prays, telling God how angry he is. After a while he begins to calm down and invites God to examine his heart. As he prays, he recalls negative remarks he made about some of his coworkers. True, their offense was far worse than his, but he hadn't exactly been an angel. As he thinks through the situation, he admits he had been worried about his job for a long time. Maybe his boss was telling the truth when he told him he was letting him go because his skills weren't up to par. By opening himself to God's Spirit in prayer and by asking to know the whole truth about what happened, this man may well discover it. He asks for pardon and for the grace to forgive those who've hurt him. His honesty and his magnanimity toward those who have hurt him, made possible by God's grace, act as a shield against bitterness, enabling him to learn and grow. Instead of becoming imprisoned by bitter memories, he transcends them and experiences healing.

As Volf points out, "We are not just shaped *by* memories: we ourselves *shape* the memories that shape us." It is possible to load our memories with falsehoods, to skew them in a way that makes the person or people who have hurt us look even worse than they are. It is also possible to remember in a way that denies any responsibility we may bear. Memory can inflate the wrong, painting the perpetrator in demonic proportions at the same time it depicts us as more saintly and peace-loving than we are.

EXAMINING OURSELVES

I have a friend who refused to speak to her son for several years. It wasn't until he became seriously ill that the two finally reconciled. I know a woman who died without ever knowing her grandchildren because years before she had done something to offend her son. He retaliated by forbidding her any contact with her grandchildren. All of us know couples who prefer to blame each other rather than admit their part in a divorce. And who hasn't seen children locked in sibling rivalry, each giving back as good as they get? Year after year the insults pile up until they form a great big mountain of hurt that can never be scaled or conquered.

But by the grace of God they can be conquered. The first step is the hardest, because it involves telling the truth to the people who least want to hear it—ourselves. We have to be willing to be ruthlessly honest about our part in a conflict, determined to take the "plank" out of our own eye before trying to withdraw the "speck" from our neighbor's. Even if our share of the blame is miniscule, it still needs to be acknowledged and examined. Why? Because the truth we discover is precious. It has the potential to reshape our memories in a way that can lead to peace. As Volf points out, "Only *truthful* memories give access to the event with which peace needs to be made."

Certainly there are cases in which people are entirely innocent —the child who is abused, the woman who's been mugged, the man who is hit by a drunk driver. But when it comes to many of our most hurtful memories, the picture may be more mixed. Here's an example from daily life. Say that my children tend to do things they know they shouldn't and that they repeat these infractions over and over (they do). Say that I tend to fly off the handle (I do). Say that they react to my anger with righteous indignation, pointing out that their mother has lost it and is talking to them in a way she shouldn't (they do). Over and over the offenses swing back and forth. I get upset and my children get upset. If I never calm down and admit my part in what has happened, it will be difficult for my children to admit theirs. Each of us needs to build on the truth of what *we* have done in order to resolve the issue and restore peace in our family.

Now imagine a family in which these truths are never acknowledged. The arguments build up for years on end with no one ever taking responsibility. Such a family will rarely know peace because each person will blame someone else in the family. Forgetting their own offense, they will remember only what others have done to them. Such memories, built on half truths, are evil confections that will ruin our emotional and spiritual health if we continue to indulge them.

Recently, as I was mulling over this challenge to remember rightly by remembering truthfully, I asked God if there were memories I needed to revisit. (I didn't think there were, so it was easy to ask.) One night, while I was drifting off to sleep, I began thinking about an old friend. Maggie and I had worked together during the early years of my career. At one time we had even shared an apartment. But living in close proximity did nothing to enhance our friendship. For reasons I cannot now remember, I began to feel annoyed whenever I was around her. Though I tried to hide my feelings, I often became irritable. One day, out of the blue, Maggie yelled at me, telling me in no uncertain terms how rotten I'd been to her. Then she demanded I leave, immediately. I hadn't realized how hurt she felt because we had never once discussed it. If she had come to me earlier, we might have resolved the issue. But now her anger was explosive. I was shocked. I'd never had anyone talk to me the way she did that day. Certain that her offense was way out of proportion to my own, I couldn't wait to leave.

Since then, we've kept in touch off and on over the years. Though we've maintained a veneer of friendship, I've brushed off most of her attempts to get together. As I lay in bed that night, thinking about Maggie, I realized that I had never taken responsibility for my part of the conflict. I had been rude, judgmental, and insensitive, and though I had quickly apologized when confronted with my behavior, I had never sincerely asked her forgiveness for the way I had treated her. That night, as I focused on my offenses, asking God to forgive me, I felt something release inside me. A knot was untied and my resentment dissolved. The next day, I decided to contact Maggie to see if we could share a meal together sometime soon. I wanted to apologize, sincerely, for offenses I had committed more than thirty years ago.

A few days later we shared a pleasant lunch. During the course of our time together, Maggie told me about difficulties in her early life that helped me understand where some of her rough edges had come from. When I asked her forgiveness for how I had treated her so many years ago, she seemed completely surprised, unable to remember the fact that there had ever been tensions. (Apparently there are advantages to waiting more than thirty years to say you're sorry.) For my part, I left the restaurant that day with a greater openness to continuing the friendship, freed from the resentment I had felt for so many years.

REJECTING THE ROLE OF VICTIM

What if we examine our hearts and find no fault there? Surely there are those among us who are innocent. People who've been treated with contempt merely because of their skin color, their age, or their sex, or because of the misfortune of falling prey to abuse. Even for these, it is unhealthy and dangerous to accept the role of victim for any length of time. As Miroslav Volf points out, "Victims will often become perpetrators precisely *on account of* their memories. It is *because they remember past* victimization that they feel justified in committing present violence. Or rather, it is because they remember their past victimization that they justify as rightful self-protection what to most observers looks like violence born of intolerance or even hatred. So easily does the protective shield of memory morph into a sword of violence ... Remembering wrongs will forge an identity, but the identity may be that of a person imprisoned in his own past and condemned to repeat it."

We needn't minimize or deny the scope of the wrongs we have suffered in order to reject the role of victim. Admitting these and giving ourselves time to deal honestly with the sins of others is part of the healing process. Still, defining ourselves entirely by what we have suffered will prevent us from becoming who we are in Christ. We cannot be both victim and victor as Christ calls us to be. We cannot appropriate the freedom he offers while remaining in bondage to those who have hurt us. Neither can we access his strength if we continue to give our power away to those who have oppressed us in the past. In his letter to the Romans, Paul instructs believers to clothe themselves with the Lord Jesus Christ. In Romans 12:14, 17 he tells them to "Bless those who persecute you; bless and do not curse ... Do not repay anyone evil for evil." By remembering rightly we can keep ourselves from repaying evil for evil, opening up the possibility of blessing those who persecute us.

Remembering rightly does not require that we ignore the offense, acting as though it never happened. Doing so risks harm, both to ourselves and others, because repression can achieve neither healing nor justice. In fact ignoring an offense may open the door to further abuse if the guilty person is allowed to continue unimpeded. Remembering truthfully is the first step toward justice. Again the point is not *whether* to remember but *how* to remember. We have the option of either learning the right lessons from our memories or the wrong ones.

DEALING WITH REJECTION

Some of our deepest hurts are incurred within the context of our most intimate relationships. When we give ourselves completely to another and that person loves us back, we experience bliss. But what if we give ourselves completely and meet with rejection? Or what if we are loved for a time and then abandoned? How do we deal with the memory of such rejection? How do we deal with the wounds we incur?

When trust is broken in a marriage or in a romantic relationship, we inevitably feel hurt. But the depth of our hurt and its ability to destroy us depends on where our sense of self comes from. As Christians, we are called to be rooted and grounded in Christ. His Spirit is to occupy our souls, guiding and directing, building up the life of God within us. Our self belongs only to him. But if someone else occupies that central, holy place, the loss of the relationship can destroy us.

Consider the young woman who cannot be happy without a boyfriend. As each new relationship begins, she feels elated. Finally she has found her soul mate, the one who will make her happy. But as the relationship unravels, her sense of abandonment grows. Her boyfriend may have treated her rudely, but she

140 ✦ FINDING THE PEACE GOD PROMISES

has already abused herself by allowing him to occupy the place inside her heart that belongs only to God. Each time she is jilted, she suffers wounds of abandonment and rejection, the memory of which will haunt her for many years. Ironically, as these wounds grow and fester, they will make it more difficult for her to find the love for which she longs.

Peace comes not from locating our happiness in things or in people but in being indwelt by Christ. Whether we are male or female, if our souls are occupied by anything or anyone else, God has been displaced and we will never know true *shalom*. To say it more plainly, you cannot fill a box with gold if it is already filled with clay—and we are meant to be filled with gold.

A MEMORY OF DELIVERANCE

When it comes to remembering rightly and to pursuing the peace that comes from doing so, Christians have an enormous advantage. Why? Because our faith is founded and rooted in two sacred memories, both of which have the power to shape how we interpret and remember the events of our own lives.

Imagine for a moment that you and your family have been enslaved for many years. By an extraordinary sequence of events, you have managed to escape your captors. Now you are free, able to decide the course of your life. So many choices lie ahead. One of them involves how you will remember your past enslavement. What lessons will you draw from it? Will you look back with bitterness, cursing your captors and being determined to become among those who dominate rather than those who are dominated? Or will you move forward, thankful for the gift of freedom and determined to help others who have suffered as you have?

The question before you is this: Will your dominant memory be about your enslavement, or will it be about your deliverance?

This was exactly the choice facing the Israelites after their departure from Egypt. How would they remember their bondage? As they moved into the future, would they be defined by memories of how Pharaoh had abused them or of how God had delivered them?

Fortunately for the history of the world, their faith was founded on the memory of their deliverance. Over and over in their Scriptures they praise God as the one who delivered them from their enemies. God, too, seemed fond of reminding them of this truth, repeating again and again, "I am the LORD your God, who brought you out of Egypt" (Exodus 20:2). Even their laws reflected the lessons that he wanted them to learn from their captivity.

> Love the aliens in your midst because you were once aliens.
> Help the poor because you were once poor.
> Observe the Sabbath and allow your servants to observe it because you know what it's like to be a slave never able to rest.

Even today, if you ask Jewish people which event in their Scriptures was most pivotal, most will instantly identify the exodus, because this is the one event that has most profoundly shaped their history. Instead of shaping them toward cruelty, their experience as slaves in a foreign land has often shaped them toward greater sensitivity to the needs of others.

But what does this ancient, collective memory have to do with us today? As Christians, our faith has grown from Jewish roots.

The exodus story is our story too. Like the Jews of old, we have come to know a God of mercy and power. We may have suffered greatly or perhaps only slightly. Whatever the scale of our hurt, we have the opportunity to be dominated not by the memory of what was done *to* us but by the memory of what was done *for* us. If we ask God to help us, our gratitude for his delivering hand will sooner or later eclipse the hurt we suffered. In the process of this deliverance we will find him reshaping our hearts, making us more like him as we learn to show mercy to the wounded, kindness to the poor, compassion to the stranger.

How might this work out in your own life? I have a friend whose child suffered for many years from a mental disorder before being effectively treated by medication. Over the years she has had to educate teachers, friends, and family members who have at times shown disdain for her son, little realizing that a flaw in biology and not a "bad heart" is at the root of many of his problems. At times she and her husband have felt judged by others who are clueless about the difficulty of raising a child who has a mental illness.

Recently, as she listened to the news reports of a multiple shooting by a young man with the likely diagnosis of paranoid schizophrenia, she decided to write a letter to his mother. Telling her how very sorry she was about everything that had happened, she explained that she too had a son who suffered from a mental disorder. Realizing that people tend to blame the family whenever anything goes wrong with a child, she tried to offer some solace, promising to pray for the family and their imprisoned son.

While the country was fixated on the suffering of this young man's innocent victims, as it should have been, at least one woman realized there were other casualties of this terrible tragedy. After the shootings, more than one public figure characterized this couple's son as evil and deserving of death. Though my friend wasn't in a position to judge the level of this young man's culpability, she knew that a rush to judgment helps no one. Had she not had a child who suffered from a mental illness and had she not endured the harsh judgments of others, this mother may never have thought of reaching out her hand to a stranger in a time of tremendous need.

All of us know people whose memories of suffering have shaped them toward mercy and positive action rather than toward bitterness and rage.

A Memory of Death and Resurrection

The second memory that shapes our faith as Christians is, of course, the memory of Christ's death and resurrection. In fact the passion of Jesus is closely linked to the memory of the exodus, unfolding as it did on Passover. The original Passover, you will remember, occurred on the night before the Israelites' dramatic escape from Egypt. By marking their doors with the blood of a lamb, they were spared the judgment that fell on the Egyptians. Hundreds of years later, Jesus became the lamb slain for us. But instead of delivering us from earthly enemies, Christ has saved us from bondage to sin and death. Belonging to him is a wonderful but humbling experience. We recognize that we are broken people, sinners saved by grace for a gracious purpose. Remembering ourselves in this way will make it easier to extend grace to people who have hurt us, to those who stand equally in need of Christ's grace.

Consider what the Lord told his disciples at the meal he shared with them the night before his death: *Do this in remembrance of me.* Indeed our whole lives—past, present, and future—should be lived and understood within the framework of this redemptive memory. We should do everything *in memory of him.*

A friend of mine spent many years praying with people for the healing of memories. At times it would become obvious that demonic influences had been at work in the person's past. Rather than carrying on a dramatic deliverance ministry, attempting to identify the presence of evil spirits, he spent most of his time doing what he called "praying the gospel into people's hearts." He knew that even the most horrific memories could be healed when people began to believe and take hold of what God had already done for them.

Kurt is a single father whose teenage son has been diagnosed with a severe mood disorder. Despite therapy and medication, his son still has meltdowns, making their home feel like an emotional war zone. Here's how Kurt describes his son:

"Mark is a constant challenge. Nothing pleases him, he is quick to overreact, and is always arguing with his sister. He's so impulsive that I can't leave the two of them alone for fear that Mark will get upset and do something stupid or dangerous. Believe me, I love my son, but to be honest, I wish I could send him to boarding school or place him in suspended animation for a little while just so that our lives could calm down."

Though tempted to despair, Kurt has repeatedly decided to interpret his family situation within the framework of the redemptive story he believes in. He finds solace and courage from the story of how God led his people out of Egypt, believing that he will also lead him and his son to a place of greater peace.

Refusing to give in to hopelessness, he chooses instead to believe that the God who raised Jesus from the dead is able to redeem his son as well.

Remembering rightly is a powerful tool for dealing with both the past and the present, freeing us to move into the future with greater freedom and hope. Each of us is called to interpret our own life story in light of the larger story we believe in. Because nothing is impossible for God, he can take the evil we have suffered and the pain that still afflicts us and make them into something good, for ourselves and others. If we ask his Spirit to be at work within us, he will teach us to remember rightly, reshaping our memories into a force for good and a pathway for peace.

As important as it is to learn to remember rightly, the process of healing sometimes involves taking a more drastic step. Let's look at a vital ingredient in the healing process, one that can open a pathway to peace for ourselves and even at times for those who have wronged us.

PURSUING PEACE

1. How have memories shaped your life for good? How have they shaped it for ill?
2. Miroslav Volf points out that "only *truthful* memories give access to the event with which peace needs to be made." As you pray through difficult memories, ask God for the grace to remember them truthfully. How can you build on the truth in a way that will enable God to heal you?
3. What are some of the dangers of taking on a victim mentality?

4. Spend time praying through a difficult memory in light
   of the Exodus story (Exodus 12–15) or the narrative
   of Christ's death and resurrection (Matthew 26–28).
   What happens when you do this?

Chapter 10

REIMAGINING OUR ENEMIES

Bear with each other and forgive one another
if any of you has a grievance against someone.
Forgive as the Lord forgave you.

Colossians 3:13

John Paul Lederach has spent most of his life pursuing peace in some of the most troubled regions of the world—Somalia, Columbia, Nepal, and Northern Ireland, to name a few. Central to any effort at peacemaking, he says, is the ability to imagine yourself in a relationship with your enemy. If the militant Islamic group Hamas, for instance, cannot imagine having a relationship with the Israeli government (since it doesn't admit Israel's right to exist), efforts at peace will fail. Similarly, if we can't imagine having a relationship with our enemies, our own efforts to find the peace God promises will prove fruitless.

But how does one begin to imagine such a thing, particularly if the offense has been grievous? It's one thing to imagine a relationship with a colleague who has bad-mouthed you in front of the boss, but quite another to imagine a relationship with an abusive ex-spouse. It may seem too painful and far too risky. Failing to do so, however, might be even riskier, because it places your heart in jeopardy of being destroyed by anger, bitterness, and depression.

To suggest that people imagine having a relationship with their enemy may sound like folly. How, for instance, can a woman envision a relationship with a rapist? Or how can a man envision a relationship with a thug who beat him? Isn't that the height of stupidity? Doesn't the advice sound preposterous?

One would be tempted to think so if it weren't for the words of Jesus instructing his followers to take the outrageous step of offering their cheek for yet another slap. He told them to love their enemies, to bless those who curse them.

As always, we are tempted to dismiss Christ's teaching as being too hard or impractical for ordinary people to follow. It may even sound naïve. But Jesus prevents us from ignoring him by following his own advice—and following it all the way to the cross. More than any other figure in history, Jesus was able to envision a relationship with the enemy. It was precisely this ability that made his death possible. Paul reminds the Colossians of this by saying, "Once you were alienated from God and were enemies in your minds because of your evil behavior. But now he has reconciled you by Christ's physical body through death to present you holy in his sight, without blemish and free from accusation" (Colossians 1:21–22).

According to Paul, God started this whole business by believing that his enemies could become transformed into his friends.

Listen to how he instructs believers in Rome: "Very rarely will anyone die for a righteous person, though for a good person someone might possibly dare to die. But God demonstrates his own love for us in this: While we were still sinners, Christ died for us" (Romans 5:7–8). As Christ's followers, we are to be catalysts of transformation, keeping the cycle going by imitating Jesus in our own most difficult relationships.

In some cases, envisioning a relationship with an enemy may involve having some measure of contact with the offender. This was what happened when Pope John Paul II met with Mehmet Ali Agca in an Italian prison in order to forgive him for attempting to assassinate him. It also happens when our enemy is someone we can't avoid, like a neighbor or a colleague. In other cases, it may be dangerous and foolish to have further contact, as in the case of a woman and her attacker.

What then is required? Something still painfully difficult—as victims of another's sin, we must at least imagine the possibility of forgiveness and reconciliation. To do so requires not that we drop our demand for justice, but that we repudiate our desire for vengeance. In such cases, our relationship with our enemies will primarily consist of praying for them, asking God to bless and transform them, and forgiving them from the heart whether or not they are repentant.

BRIDGING THE IMPOSSIBLE GAP

Iphigenia Mukantabana is a remarkable woman. She sits in front of her house, just an hour from Kigali, weaving baskets with her friend Epiphania Mukanyndwi. Both have something in common—a sorrow that most of us cannot imagine. They share the sadness of fellow Rwandans who survived a genocide in which nearly one million of their countrymen were massacred.

At the time of the genocide, a minister was quoted on the front cover of a magazine saying, "There are no devils left in hell, they have all gone to Rwanda." Mukantabana describes the mayhem of those days: "Women and girls were raped, and I saw it all," she says. "The men and boys were beaten and then slaughtered. They told others to dig a hole, get in, then they piled earth on top of them while they were still alive." Ordinary citizens who went to church together, whose children attended school together, who lived together as neighbors—these were the ones who were slaughtering each other.

Mukantabana lost her husband and five of her children when they were hacked to death by a mob of Hutu militants. Her friend Mukanyndwi lived through the horror as well. But it is not the thread of their common loss that ties their friendship together. In fact, Mukanyndwi is closely tied to one of the men who murdered Mukantabana's entire family—Mukanyndwi's husband. Years after the killing, the man confessed to reporters from CNN that he was part of a mob that slaughtered twenty-five people, including Mukantabana's husband and children. "We used machetes, hoes, and wooden clubs," he explained.

For four years Mukantabana could not bring herself to speak to him or his wife. There was too much hurt and mistrust. The breakthrough happened when he voluntarily went before a tribal gathering to confess his guilt and ask for forgiveness. With Christ's help, Mukantabana accepted her enemy's pleas for forgiveness.

Today the two Rwandan women, Mukantabana and Mukanyndwi, maintain a close friendship. By the power of Christ at work within her, Mukantabana has managed to bridge the impossible gap between herself and her former enemy. Amazingly, she now shares her family meals with Mukanyndwi and her husband.

This remarkable story has been repeated thousands of times across Rwanda, where those who have lost family have been able to face and forgive their murderers. Laura Waters Hinson produced a moving documentary about the process of reconciliation in Rwanda entitled *As We Forgive*. Still, much as we might wish Rwanda's problems were consigned to the past, Hinson points out that most Rwandans have not yet reconciled. "In Rwanda," she says, "they have outlawed the use of 'Tutsi' or 'Hutu.'" (The majority Hutu tribe did most of the killing of members of the minority Tutsi tribe.) "There are no ethnic identity cards anymore. But living together without forgiveness is not reconciliation. On the surface they have tried to do away with divisions, but underneath there are still a lot of hostilities."

WHAT HAPPENS WHEN YOU CHOOSE BITTERNESS

In his classic book *The Great Divorce*, C. S. Lewis takes the reader on an imaginary tour of heaven and hell. In one particularly arresting scene, he shows us how difficult it can be to imagine a relationship with our enemy, even if he has repented of the wrongs he has done. A man who has recently died and is now a ghost stands at the outskirts of heaven. There he encounters one of his former employees, a man named Len, who has been sent to escort him to heaven.

"'Well, I'm damned,' said the ghost. 'I wouldn't have believed it. It's a fair knock-out. It isn't right, Len, you know. What about poor Jack, eh?' ...

"'He is here,' said the other. 'You will meet him soon, if you stay.'

"'But you murdered him.'

"'Of course I did. It is all right now.'

"'All right, is it? All right for you, you mean. But what about the poor chap himself, laying cold and dead?'

"'But he isn't. I have told you, you will meet him soon. He sent you his love.' ... 'Murdering old Jack wasn't the worst thing I did,' Len admitted to the ghost. 'That was the work of a moment and I was half mad when I did it. But I murdered you in my heart, deliberately, for years. I used to lie awake at nights thinking what I'd do to you if I ever got the chance. That is why I have been sent to you now: to ask your forgiveness and to be your servant as long as you need one, and longer if it pleases you. I was the worst. But all the men who worked under you felt the same. You made it hard for us, you know. And you made it hard for your wife too and for your children.'

"'I'd rather be damned,' said the ghost, 'than go along with you. I came here to get my rights, see? Not to go sniveling along on charity tied onto your apron-strings. If they're too fine to have me without you, I'll go home.' It was almost happy now that it could, in a sense, threaten. 'That's what I'll do,' it repeated, 'I'll go home.' ... In the end, still grumbling, but whimpering also a little as it picked its way over the sharp grasses, it made off."

Scandalized to learn that his former employee, a murderer, had been welcomed into heaven, the ghost refused heaven and chose hell instead, unable to envision a relationship with his enemy. This is a chilling picture of what can happen to a person who neither forgives nor asks for forgiveness. Our choices have consequences here and hereafter. As Lewis says, they will define whether earth will be for us a pathway to heaven or a prelude to hell.

LEVERAGING THE PAIN OF OUR PAST

Wess Stafford is president and CEO of Compassion International, a child's advocacy ministry. His story shows us how God can "leverage the pain of our past," bringing good out of evil. The son of missionaries in Africa, Wess was sent to an isolated missionary school when he was only six years old. Unbeknownst to his parents, he and the other children were subjected to unspeakable acts of cruelty for infractions as minor as opening their eyes when they were supposed to be napping or leaving a wrinkle in a bedspread. Their persecutors threatened them, saying that their parents' ministry to the Africans would be destroyed if they ever disclosed what was happening at the school. Because Wess loved the Africans in his village, he kept silent, believing his silence would lead to their salvation.

One day, after a visit with his family to the US, just as he was about to board a plane that would transport him back to Africa and the school, he blurted out the truth to his mother. A minute later he was whisked away along with the other children before his mother could process what her son had just told her. She and Wess's father followed by boat. During the month-long journey, struggling with what her son had told her, his mother suffered a nervous collapse. When the staff at the school caught wind of what had caused her breakdown, they became enraged.

Hauling him in front of his classmates, one of the house

parents forced ten-year-old Wess to stand on a chair and then handed him a birthday candle with a wick at both ends. "Children," he announced, "you cannot serve both God and Satan. Wesley has tried. You cannot burn a candle at both ends without getting burned. Watch what happens when you try." Then he lit the match.

In that moment, Wess received his calling. "As flames licked closer to my skin, from deep within me arose a gust of strength I cannot fully explain to this day," he says. "I had a desperate thought: I could *win this time* ... if I could endure enough pain ... I felt the evil and injustice to the core of my soul. I was not Satan's tool. I was a little boy with a broken heart who had found his voice and cried out for rescue. So, enough — enough shame, enough abuse, enough lies. It had to stop somewhere, sometime. I made my decision: It stops now! I'm not letting go!

"Nothing was going to make me cry out or drop that candle. This is where I would take my stand — this was my little Masada.

"I shook violently, tears brimming in anticipation of burned flesh ... All I could hear was the pulsing of blood in my ears. I clenched my teeth, tightened every muscle in my body, and pinched the candle as fiercely as I could. I stared as the edges of my fingers turned red. A blister popped up. I was transported out of my body. I floated above this terrified boy, watching as if it were happening to someone else ...

"Just then, a child in the front row couldn't stand it any longer, and he jumped and slapped the candle out of my hand ... The meeting was over. But standing there alone on my chair, I had received my *calling*. In an instant, I had gone from victim to victor. From that day forward, I would protect children. I would forever speak up for those who cannot speak for themselves."

Asked how he moved from pain to deliverance, he answers: "At age seventeen, I realized that those who hurt me would never apologize. They weren't even sorry. But I could no longer bear carrying the pain of my past, so I chose to forgive them anyway. 'Get out of my heart. Get out of my mind. Get out of my life!' I remember saying. 'What you did to me will not define me. You stole my childhood, but you cannot have the rest of my life. Get out—I forgive you!' "

At that moment he learned to stand up against evil and then to transcend it through the power of forgiveness. Wess leveraged his painful past and has since used it to champion vulnerable children throughout the world.

Forgiving the "Beloved Enemy"

Until now we have been speaking of forgiveness for major offenses. But what about the thousands of smaller offenses committed against us throughout the course of our lives? Few of us will have the opportunity of granting forgiveness on any kind of grand scale. CNN will probably never pester us for an interview, offering us a stage on which to express our magnanimity. Instead, our challenge is to make both repentance and forgiveness part of the fabric of our daily lives. Why? Because sin is so daily.

Some of the most difficult offenses to forgive, whether they are large or small, are those committed by people I call "beloved enemies," the people we live with, work with, and attend church with—the people we care most about. Family and friends have the ability to hurt us in ways that strangers often do not. For one thing, they know us well. That means they are aware of our vulnerabilities. For another, we are in far more frequent contact with them. As a result their offenses can pile up. It's one thing to forgive a past offense but quite another to forgive something that has happened more than once and that might happen again in the future. The husband who has a habit of belittling his wife; the mother who berates her children; the teenager who pushes every boundary in sight—habitual offenses can take time and effort to change.

In Matthew 18:21 Peter asks Jesus how many times he should forgive someone who sins against him, tentatively suggesting that perhaps seven times would be about right. This would have sounded quite generous to Peter and his contemporaries. But Jesus does not commend his star pupil for answering correctly. Instead, he replies, "I tell you, not seven times, but seventy-seven times." The note in the NIV Bible suggests an alternate translation of "*seventy times seven*," which is 490 times! But the advice Jesus gives Peter is even more extreme than this. By using the phrase "seventy-seven times," Jesus is deliberately alluding to the only other place in the Bible where this particular phrase appears.

You may remember that the first murder is recorded in the fourth chapter of the Bible, which tells the story of Cain and his unfortunate brother, Abel. Then, in Genesis 4:23–24 we meet one of Cain's ill-tempered descendants, a man by the name of Lamech, who promises to pay back his enemies not just seven times (a number of completeness in the Bible) but seventy-seven times. Clearly, Lamech's thirst for revenge went far beyond anything that would have been considered fair or complete by his contemporaries. By repeating the distinctive phrase "seventy-seven times," Jesus was invoking the story of Lamech, only he was advocating a complete reversal, implying that his disciples should let their forgiveness exceed what anyone else might think of as complete or fair. They were to forgive lavishly, generously, persistently.

The forgiveness Christ advocated and practiced is disarming, surprising, and creative, opening paths to peace both inside the one who forgives and inside the one who is forgiven.

Do you remember the story of one of the Bible's most dysfunctional families? It's the story of Joseph and the brothers who sold him into slavery (Genesis 37; 39–50). The roots of the story stretch back into family history, with a dynamic of favoritism that began with Abraham, continued with Isaac, and then carried on into the life of Jacob. This plague of favoritism reached its apex with Jacob's preference for Joseph above all Jacob's older sons. Consumed by jealousy, the sons conspired to sell their brother into slavery.

In one of the great reversals of history, Joseph, the slave, becomes a man of wisdom and power, a great ruler in Egypt. His unwitting brothers come to Joseph during a famine, begging for bread. In one of Genesis's most memorable scenes, Joseph reveals himself to his brothers, saying, "I am your brother Joseph, the one you sold into Egypt! And now, do not be distressed and do not be angry with yourselves for selling me here, because it was to save lives that God sent me ahead of you. For two years now there has been famine in the land, and for the next five years there will be no plowing and reaping. But God sent me ahead of you to preserve for you a remnant on earth and to save your lives by a great deliverance" (Genesis 45:4–7).

Notice how Joseph reframes the memory of his painful exile, placing it within the context of God's larger purposes. Then he treats his treacherous brothers with shocking grace, extending forgiveness and welcome. Joseph's gesture is so unexpected and so powerful that it has far-reaching effects, helping to halt the transmission of the family sin of favoritism to future generations. Finally, the "beloved enemy" has been transformed into the beloved.

FORGIVING OURSELVES

For some of us the most difficult person to forgive is not a brother, a cousin, or a father. It is not a sister, a mother, or a daughter. It is someone even closer. It is ourselves. There may be several reasons why we find it hard to forgive ourselves. Certainly one is that we may have a self-image problem. I am not suggesting we are suffering from low self-esteem. On the contrary, our problem may have more to do with high self-esteem. We may be suffering from an idealized view of ourselves that is out of line with reality. Because we think we are better than we are, we are disappointed when we do not live up to our standards, punishing ourselves emotionally for our failures and being unable to extend to ourselves the grace we extend to others.

One of the pitfalls of belonging to Christ is that God sometimes does such a good job of cleaning us up that we may forget how desperately we still need him. In my case, I began my Christian life with an acute awareness of my need. But as I followed Christ, I began growing in confidence. Gradually, old habits were shed and new and healthier ones were formed. Wounds were healed. I began using gifts I didn't even know I had. As life improved, I became more self-confident and self-reliant.

Because my conversion had been fairly dramatic, I tended to see my life in "before" and "after" terms. After a while, my pre-Christian self receded into the past, gradually becoming someone

I remembered but barely recognized. Where I had once felt desperate for God's forgiveness and saving grace, I now felt fairly good about my life. I knew what I was supposed to do and I tried my best to do it. Without realizing it, my brand of Christianity began morphing into something that depended much more on me than it did on God. But all my trying didn't result in a life of peace and joy. Instead, I felt increasingly frustrated, and God seemed increasingly remote.

As always, Christ was merciful, letting me come to the end of my own strength so that I could recognize that twenty years after my conversion, I was still as desperate for his grace and mercy as when his love first swept over me. In addition to recognizing my own self-image problem, it became clear that I also had a God-image problem, a failure to believe that God was really as good as I had once thought he was.

Maybe that's what Christ meant when he exhorted the church in Ephesus, "Yet I hold this against you: You have forsaken the love you had at first. Consider how far you have fallen!" (Revelation 2:4–5).

Our first love wasn't built on our efforts to be perfect, to follow all the rules. It was pure gift, lavished on us because we were for the first time living in reality, seeing ourselves as broken people in the midst of a broken world, in desperate need of grace. God heard us, forgave us, and filled us with his Spirit. That's the "height" from which we have fallen, the height of knowing how good God is, how fiercely he loves us, and how well he wants to provide for us.

Our conversion isn't meant to be only a one-time event, something we merely look back on with wonder. Living in God's grace, admitting our need, becoming like him by the power of his

Spirit—these are to be hallmarks of our lives as Christians. We are the branches, connected to the vine from which our life flows. As we practice the kind of "seven-times-seventy" forgiveness that Jesus urges, we will finally become to ourselves what we already are to Christ—beloved men and women for whom he died and rose.

The peace God promises is not just for the tough times or the extraordinary circumstances. Indeed, God promises us his peace in our day-to-day lives as well. In the next section, we will look at how we can pursue peace in practical ways: through taming our tongue, caring for our bodies, ridding ourselves of encumbrances, and adopting an attitude of joy and thanksgiving. Peace can be found every day—when we walk the path with Jesus.

PURSUING PEACE

1. How did Jesus envision having a relationship with his enemies? How can you envision a relationship with your own enemies?
2. Think about your own "beloved enemies." Why is it sometimes difficult to extend forgiveness to those who are closest to you?
3. Do you find it difficult to forgive yourself, unable to extend to yourself the grace you extend to others? How might you benefit from realizing the extent of your brokenness and your continuing need for grace?
4. Who have you asked for forgiveness? Who do you still need to ask for forgiveness?

Part Four

PEACE IN THE DAY-TO-DAY

My son, do not forget my teaching, but keep my

commands in your heart, for they will prolong your life

many years and bring you peace and prosperity.

Proverbs 3:1–2

Chapter 11 ❧

TAMING
THE TONGUE

> *Remind the people ... to be obedient, to be*
> *ready to do whatever is good, to slander no*
> *one, to be peaceable and considerate, and*
> *always to be gentle toward everyone.*
>
> Titus 3:1–2

Lecturing to a crowd in Denver one day, Rabbi Joseph Telushkin looked out at the audience and asked: "How many of you grew up in a household in which somebody's ill temper had a bad effect on the household?"

To Telushkin's surprise one person in the audience immediately raised her hand, and then another hand shot up right next to hers. Why the surprise? The first hand belonged to his six-year-old daughter and the second to her younger sister, both of whom happened to be in the audience that day. His listeners, of course, were amused and delighted by his children's display of honesty.

It's a courageous admission, especially from an author who wrote a book entitled *Words That Hurt, Words That Heal*. What's the moral of the story? Here's what I take away from it. If you are going to dispense advice in a public place, make sure your children are nowhere in the vicinity! Come to think of it, if you are the author of a book about peace and one of your chapters is entitled "Taming the Tongue," it may be smart to hide the book lest your children discover it one day and begin revealing your own deficiencies in the area of speech.

Family life brings with it many benefits, not the least of which is that children help to keep you honest regarding your struggles and challenges. To learn to speak words that consistently bring peace instead of distress would, indeed, be a great blessing.

SPEECH DISORDERS

We know that when sin first entered the world, many of the good things God made became distorted and corrupted. Gifts, abilities, and desires that he intended for our good and the good of his created world began operating in dysfunctional ways, bringing pain and suffering in their wake. Our sex drive is a notable example. Good in itself, sexual desire has become so distorted in some people that it has destroyed the peace in irretrievable ways.

Similarly, the gift of language, the power to communicate and connect with others, though a unique and wonderful ability, has often brought with it immense suffering. Unlike sexual dysfunction, speech disorders affect every one of us because nobody uses their tongue in the way God intended, at least not all of the time. Neither have we escaped the trauma that someone else's ungoverned tongue can inflict. How can we learn not only to constrain the negative power of speech but to unleash its power to bless and heal?

Think for a moment about your favorite restaurant. What makes it so special? Certainly the food and the way it's cooked. But what keeps you going back? For many of us, it's the ambiance. The design, the lighting, the smells, the background music, the level of service—all these create a unique atmosphere. Speech, too, creates a certain ambiance. Entering a room, we can often sense whether the atmosphere is upbeat, encouraging, and relaxed or whether it is anxious, depressed, and angry.

Have you ever been house hunting when you sense that one house just feels better than another? It seems happier. Or conversely when a house feels sad or depressed? Chronic negative speech creates an atmosphere that is both painful and hazardous to the spiritual and emotional health of everyone in range. It's like breathing in secondary smoke. The ill effects of speech that is powered by anger, negativity, or depression take a heavy toll.

I remember overhearing a babysitter trying to console one of my childhood playmates who had just been taunted by her older brother. "Don't worry," she said, taking the girl in her arms. "Sticks and stones may break your bones but words will never hurt you." The babysitter meant well, but I recognized this saying for the canard that it is. Words have an incredible power to hurt and damage.

"What are you, stupid?" an exasperated father blurts out to a son who has just presented him with failing grades. "You're a lazy, selfish brat," shouts a mother to her teenage daughter. "Stop nagging, you old cow," snaps a husband whose wife has reminded him one-too-many times about a chore he promised to do. In the heat of the moment, all of us have sometimes been guilty of lobbing words like little grenades. Though we may later repent of our unkindness, we cannot simply retract words that have lodged like shrapnel in the hearts and minds of those who've heard them.

How much better to prevent the damage in the first place by heeding this simple Amish proverb: "Swallowing words before you say them is so much better than having to eat them afterward." Learning to hold our tongues not only prevents irreparable harm, but it can even make us appear wiser than we are. As the book of Proverbs so bluntly puts it, "Even fools are thought wise when they keep silent; with their mouths shut, they seem intelligent" (Proverbs 17:28 NLT).

PAY ATTENTION TO YOUR SPEECH

Where can we find the power to change, to harness the power of our tongues? Psalm 34:12–14 advises:

> *Whoever of you loves life*
> *and desires to see many good days,*
> *keep your tongue from evil*
> *and your lips from telling lies.*
> *Turn from evil and do good;*
> *seek peace and pursue it.*

The message is clear. If you want to have a good life, begin paying attention to your speech.

What can we learn about the power of words from looking at Scripture and the life of Jesus? Have you ever wondered why the Bible repeatedly refers to him as the Word? Doesn't the "Word of God," in contrast to the "Lamb of God" or the "King of Kings," for instance, sound rather esoteric? It does until you understand that Jesus is called the Word because he perfectly communicates God to us. If you ever get confused by certain Old Testament images of God that make him seem mean and wrathful, you have only to look at the life of Jesus to understand who God is and how he loves you. Though Jesus communicated through his words, he also spoke to us through all the events of his life. Everything about him—his birth, his miracles, his parables, his life, his death, and his resurrection—all these express the mind and heart of God to us.

What's more, Jesus had an uncanny power with words. Consider a few examples:

- [Jesus] *said* to the paralyzed man, "Get up, take your mat and go home." (Matthew 9:6)
- [Jesus] *said* to the waves, "Quiet! Be still!" (Mark 4:39)
- Jesus *called* in a loud voice, "Lazarus, come out!" (John 11:43)

Now let's turn to the very first book of the Bible. Listen to how Genesis 1 depicts God creating the world:

- And God *said*, "Let there be light," and there was light. (Genesis 1:3)
- And God *said*, "Let the water under the sky be gathered to one place, and let dry ground appear." And it was so. (1:9)
- God *said*, "Let the land produce vegetation ..." And it was so. (1:11)

Do you see the parallels? God created the world simply by speaking it into being. Jesus re-creates it through his miracles of healing and restoration. With a word he shows his mastery over creation by stilling the storm at sea. As creatures made in God's image, we are called to participate in his life-giving work by using our own words in creative and redemptive ways. Though Jesus is uniquely the Word, our own words are also endowed with creative power. As believers, we can help to bring worlds into being that reflect a measure of peace and hope rather than the stress and chaos of the world around us.

A teacher who encourages a child to believe she can succeed, a wife who makes a point of commending her husband whenever she can, a man who tells his son he loves him no matter what—all these speak words that can be pivotal in another's life. Even small words can make a big difference to the people we encounter in the course of our day—the bank trainee who's slowing things down, the clerk who bags our groceries, the person who sits at the desk next to ours. Even words of correction, if they are spoken wisely and in a spirit of love, can be words that bless and bring peace.

LEARN TO INTERPRET

In his book *War of Words*, Paul Tripp tells of an incident that displays the everyday challenges we face when it comes to speaking rightly. Tripp had been looking forward to a pleasant day off when two of his children began fighting. He had been reading when the quarrel broke out. Here's how he described his frame of mind as their verbal taunts escalated: "Didn't they know what my life is like? Didn't they know how hard I worked for them? Didn't they realize how important this day was to me? Couldn't they see I was trying to read? Couldn't they figure out that this was the kind of stuff that wrecks days like this?

"In that spirit I got up and marched toward the scene. I saw my daughter first. I spoke to her out of my sense that I had been personally wronged, that she was wrecking *my* day, and that she didn't seem to care. I gave her the 'I do and do for you and this is the thanks I get, why don't you grow up for once?' speech. My words were accusatory and harsh, born more out of a love for myself than for her."

"The problem with the way I spoke to my daughter," Tripp says, "was that I entered the room as if I were God, rather than a man under God's authority, with a heartfelt desire to see his will done in my life *and* my daughter's."

Who can't identify with the story of this frustrated father? Let's consider what was going on in the interaction they had. As Tripp points out, he lost control of his speech not because of the way he responded to the *facts* of the situation but because of the way he *interpreted* those facts. He had felt cheated out of a well-deserved day of rest. Surely his children could show a little consideration. That's the interpretation that powered his anger.

It's the same with us. How we *interpret* the facts of any given situation will determine our response to them. If we want to speak in ways that create a world of peace rather than one of strife, we need to begin by tuning into the stories we are telling ourselves because these are what will determine the quality of the words that come out of our mouths. These internal narratives can develop quickly. Our boss fails to greet us in the morning and we conclude she's unhappy with the report we turned in yesterday. But maybe she's simply preoccupied. Our children yell at each other, and we conclude they're hopeless. They will be at each other's throats for as long as they live. But perhaps God wants us to resist giving up on them so that we can help them find better ways to relate.

When you feel yourself getting annoyed, when your irritation starts to rise, try asking yourself what exactly is bothering you. Why do you feel so put out? Force yourself to stop and consider what's going on inside your head. Are you reacting out of selfishness or out of concern for others? It's hard to argue with Paul Tripp's contention that "in the heart of every sinner is a desire that life would be a resort." When I trace the roots of my own irritability, I often discover it arises from disappointed expectations. I want things to go a certain way. I don't want anyone rocking my comfortable boat.

SELF-CONTROL
AND SLOWING OUR RESPONSE TIME

Sometimes, of course, the roots of our discontent are more basic. They don't arise from any particular story we're telling ourselves but rather from something far simpler. We're irritable because we're tired or our feet ache or our head feels like someone just took a hammer to it. That's when our reptilian brain can kick in, causing us to react in self-defensive ways.

Speaking of reptilian brains, you may find yourself reacting to provocation at the speed of light. For instance, you may be a person who tends to step into a conflict rather than stepping back from it. If you're like me, you may find it hard to walk into the other room for a few moments before you respond. Doing so can take tremendous self-control, but isn't self-control one part of the fruit of the Holy Spirit (Galatians 5:22–23)? If we seek to conform our lives to Christ, surely the Spirit will give us the help we need to grow in self-mastery.

James counseled believers to "be quick to listen, slow to speak and slow to become angry" (James 1:19). Here's how The Message paraphrases this passage: "Post this at all the intersections, dear friends: Lead with your ears, follow up with your tongue, and let anger straggle along in the rear." What a great visual! Perhaps we should post this passage on the refrigerator, the bathroom mirror, and the dashboard of our car. If we want to raise the level of peace in our lives, we need to heed this important directive.

Unless it's imperative that we intervene quickly, it's usually wise to try to slow our response time. Doing so will give us the opportunity to cool off and examine the stories we are telling ourselves. If we can manage to wait even five minutes, we will often respond with greater calm and care. Slowing our response time also gives us space to listen to the other person's explanation without our emotional reaction distorting it. Even when we mess up, we can still learn from our mistakes, reviewing the narrative that was developing in our minds right before we lost control.

Paul Tripp offers another example that can guide our response to those we love: "When you're taking a vacation and the children are quarreling in the back seat, there is more going on than your expensive vacation being ruined! The need for restoration is revealing itself. You can respond to this situation as an irritated parent or as a restorer who wants to be used by the great Restorer … God is calling you to more than self-pity. He has positioned you to be a restorer." We need to keep this truth constantly in mind whether we are having words with our children, our spouse, or our boss. God can use our words for the good of others.

FRUITLESS WORDS

Though our words often exert more influence than we might imagine, they are certainly not all-powerful. One of the biggest parenting mistakes I have made is to expect my words to do more than they were designed to do. Let me explain. Contrary to what our children might think, most of us don't wake up in the morning itching for the chance to discipline them. We would much rather reason with them, hoping our wise words will persuade them to behave. But words don't always work in the way we intend. Sometimes we talk too much and act too little.

When I was in middle school, my mother would wake my sister and me with a kiss and then tell each of us in a gentle voice, "Darling, it's time to get up." But her kind words rarely made for peaceful mornings because Sue and I would simply roll over and go back to sleep, trusting that after ten minutes had elapsed, she would shout up the stairs: "SUE! ANN! GET UP NOW! YOU'RE GOING TO BE LATE FOR SCHOOL!" Our mornings might have passed more peacefully had my mother simply let us suffer the consequences of being late a couple of times.

Come to think of it, I nagged my daughter every morning of her first-grade year because she took so long to get ready. At the end of that school year, when all the awards were being passed out, she received one for never being tardy. I was shocked! My daughter receiving a reward for being on time? It was unthinkable. I wanted to push past all the seven-year-olds in attendance and grab that award for myself. After all, I was the one who deserved it! All that prodding and reminding her day in and day out had been so stressful. Little wonder that I still have to drive her to school sometimes. Even though she's now in high school, my millions of words, whether spoken calmly or yelled in frustration, have still not resulted in her reliably rolling out of bed on time to catch the bus.

Even though our words can fail to achieve the results we desire, they still retain tremendous power, though this power is often released in unintentional ways. My habit of nagging my first grader, for instance, simply made the morning more frustrating and stressful for the entire family. Samuel Levenson has remarked that insanity is hereditary. "You get it from your kids," he said. I couldn't agree more. But I also have to agree with the person who pointed out that insanity is doing the same thing over and over and expecting different results. As Paul Tripp points out, "A parent must not be so afraid of what will happen to his child that he tries to do with words what only God can accomplish by his grace." Expecting too much from our words can result in nagging and yelling, whether at our children or others.

GUARDING AGAINST GOSSIP

In Colossians 3:12, Paul says: "Therefore, as God's chosen people, holy and dearly loved, clothe yourselves with compassion, kindness, humility, gentleness and patience." When it comes to our speech, Tripp points out, "Gentleness doesn't mean compromising the truth. Rather it means keeping the truth from being compromised by harshness and insensitivity."

Lashon hara is the Hebrew term for "evil speech." It encompasses gossip, slander, and malicious speech. It even includes saying something true that lowers the status of the person about whom it is said. More than most people, Jews have come to understand how evil speech can prepare the way for atrocities, private and public. To paraphrase an ancient Jewish proverb, "The gossiper stands in New York and kills in Chicago." Truly, *lashon hara* is murderous speech. If it does not kill people, it destroys their reputation. Worse yet, it afflicts at least three people: the person who says it, the one who listens to it, and the one whom it is said about.

According to Jewish ethics, the only time you are allowed to say something negative but truthful about someone is when the information is needed by the person to whom you are speaking. For instance, you might disclose something negative to a person considering going into business with a dishonest or incompetent person. Or you would warn someone if they were at risk of harm or danger. I was grateful, for instance, when a friend warned me about my choice of a primary care physician. As a nurse, she was familiar with many of the medical practices in town. Though she had heard nothing negative about my doctor, it was widely known that his partner was an alcoholic. What would happen, my friend asked, if I had a medical emergency and my physician was out of town? His partner would be the one calling the shots.

Even implying something negative about someone is off limits. As the Amish say, "Blessed are they who have nothing to say, and who cannot be persuaded to say it." Though gossip can be an entertaining way of passing the time, Joseph Telushkin points out that the main reason people gossip is to raise their status by lowering someone else's. To make his point, he observes that people rarely gossip about their cleaning lady. Instead, they talk about their social equals or their social superiors because gossip is primarily a status game. Bring down the status of someone on your level or above you, and your own status goes up. But gossip also alienates you from those you gossip about. Even friends may begin to wonder what you are saying about them behind their backs.

Sometimes we speak ill of others who have hurt or offended us not because we are playing the status game but because we're afraid to confront them directly. So we deliver an indirect payback by spreading negative things about them. In such cases, it's likely that we are venting to people who can't do anything to help us resolve the problem. We need to deal directly with the person who caused the issue, assuming, of course, that it is safe to do so. Doing otherwise is like confiding your symptoms to an electrician whenever you feel sick. Though he may listen sympathetically, he can't do anything to help you.

CAREFUL CRITICISM

At times each of us will have an obligation to correct others—our children, our students, a friend who is heading in the wrong direction. But when you find it necessary to deliver criticism, do your best to do it kindly, thoughtfully, and privately. Joseph Telushkin says that our goal should be "to find a way of criticizing that will inflict the minimum of hurt while doing the maximum of good."

Before you speak, he says, you should ask yourself how you feel about delivering the criticism. Does it bring you pleasure or pain? "If you realize that part of you relishes speaking out," he says, "you probably shouldn't. The insincerity of your concern, your pleasure at seeing your victim's discomfort, and/or your desire to hurt someone at whom you might be angry will probably be apparent. As a result, your listener probably will react defensively, and be unlikely to change." Criticism that is guided by love and concern is more likely to receive a positive reception.

When discussing a problem with someone, it's often best to choose a straightforward approach, speaking directly to that person about the problem. But sometimes another, more creative approach is needed. If we pray about a difficult interaction, God may inspire us with a uniquely effective way of dealing with it. Telushkin tells a delightful story about a nineteenth-century rabbi who found a creative way to approach a difficult situation. One day the rabbi decided to stop at the home of a wealthy bank manager. When the rabbi was ushered into the man's house, he sat down without a word and continued sitting there for some time without saying anything. Finally the rabbi stood up to leave.

Puzzled by the silence of his visitor, the bank manager inquired about the purpose of his visit. The rabbi explained that Jewish sages taught that just as you were commanded to say what would be listened to, you were also commanded *not* to say what wouldn't be listened to. "Now if I remain in my house and you remain in yours, I can't refrain from telling you what you will not listen to. So I had to come to your house in order to refrain from speaking it."

His curiosity piqued, the bank manager pressed him, asking him to please tell him whatever it was that he was refraining to say. Finally the rabbi relented. "Very well," he said. "A certain penniless widow owes your bank quite a sum for the mortgage of her house. Within a few days, your bank is going to dispose of her house by public sale, and she will be out on the street. I had wanted to ask you to overlook her debt, but didn't, because I knew you would not listen."

Astonished, the banker exclaimed, "But what do you expect me to do? Surely you realize that the debt is not owed to me personally, but to the bank and I am only its manager, and not its owner, and the debt runs into several hundreds, and if ..."

"It's exactly as I said all along," the rabbi replied, "that you would not want to hear."

With that he left the banker's house.

Unable to dislodge the rabbi's words from his heart, the bank manager finally relented, deciding to pay the widow's debt out of his own pocket.

RECEIVING CRITICISM

The only thing more difficult that criticizing others with kindness and sensitivity is to receive criticism well ourselves. This summer someone I didn't know delivered a stinging criticism after talking with me for about two minutes about a situation I was dealing with. She had no knowledge of me and had never met me before, but she felt qualified to pass judgment. I was surprised by her words but made a conscious decision to stay calm. I thanked her for her point of view and later shared it with close friends, explaining that I wanted to try to learn from the criticism. Did they think it was on the mark? I confess I was relieved to discover they didn't, but I had truly wanted to be open to the woman's perspective because I have come to realize that every kernel of truth, no matter how it is delivered, is to be treasured.

Had that happened to me twenty years ago, my response would have been far different. I would have been hurt and angry, instantly on the defensive. Though I dislike criticism as much as anyone, I have learned that God can use even twisted words to communicate truth to me because sometimes the person I perceive to be my adversary is the teacher I most need to learn from. I also know that I am as broken and in need of grace as anyone. Because God loves me, I also know that he is at work in all circumstances for my good. If I have already admitted my brokenness, I don't have to protect myself when someone points out one of my many imperfections.

RIGHTEOUS INDIGNATION AND RAGE

When it comes to the words we speak, some of us have fallen into a pernicious snare. Instead of taking our cues from our Christian faith, we've taken them from popular culture, which seems to have forgotten how to engage in civil discourse. Like certain television and radio pundits, we've adopted narratives that cast political parties and politicians as evil, self-serving, and uncaring. Everyone who opposes our political viewpoint gets tossed into the same basket, and we use every opportunity to vilify them. Instead of letting God's Spirit shape our hearts and attitudes, we model our speech on how the media speaks about people. Why do we resort to such tactics, sometimes becoming addicted to feelings of righteous indignation and rage? Because it's useful, at least in the short term.

Rage can hide the disappointment we feel about our own circumstances. And it can empower us when we might otherwise feel vulnerable, unable to control the events that impact us. But this kind of anger, which can extend to our work environment, our church, and our family, alienates us from others, even those who might otherwise share our views. Being around a person who is chronically angry, even if their anger is not directed at us, is like being around someone throwing fistfuls of garbage. We get smeared just by being in the vicinity.

How can we begin to tame the power of our tongues? Paul tells the Ephesians to "be angry without sinning" (4:26 GW). Paul knows we'll get angry. Sometimes it's right to be angry. But how can we be angry without sinning? A few simple things will help us. We've already talked about responding more slowly to situations that provoke us. Shut the door, take a walk, breathe in and breathe out. Try to calm down and then respond.

We can also avoid exaggerating someone else's offense. When you're angry, it's easy to lose perspective, casting someone who has hurt you in the worst possible light. But if I say that you're an inconsiderate bum, you are not likely to respond by saying, "Yes, dear, I see what you mean. I really do need to treat you more considerately." Instead, you will probably become angry and defensive, providing fuel for the argument to continue. Anger can make us forget the goal. We become far more interested in inflicting hurt than in resolving problems.

Whenever possible, we should also try to *explain* rather than *accuse*. For instance, instead of expressing a judgment by saying, "You are so selfish; you never think about me but only about what you want," you could explain how your spouse's words or actions have affected you. "When you make decisions without consulting me, it makes me feel as though you don't care what I think." Accusations will usually ramp up the anger, while explanations may help fence it in.

Anger is like water that gets into a house, spreading from room to room. The leak may have started in the roof but before you know it there's water pooling in the living room. Unless you take care of the problem quickly, the damage to your home can be devastating.

Likewise, anger tends to flood every area of a relationship. This happens when we let anger over one thing make us angry about other things. A wife, for instance, may speak ill of her husband in public. When they get home, her husband tells her how angry her comments have made him. So far that's a reasonable response. But the husband is so angry that he moves quickly to something else that's been bothering him. "You're just like your father," he says. "That man never has a kind word for anyone. Come to think of it, there's no pleasing anyone in your family."

Perhaps the husband does have a problem with his in-laws, but if he brings the matter up now, when he's already angry, the issue at hand will not be resolved, and what started as a skirmish may erupt into war. Joseph Telushkin wisely advises that we limit the expression of our anger to the incident that provoked it. If we stick to the problem at hand, regardless of the other's response, we can keep our own anger from spreading, causing us to say things we may later regret. If there are other problems in a relationship, these need to be dealt with separately, at another time.

WORDS OF HEALING AND HELP

Proverbs 12:18 says, "The words of the reckless pierce like swords, but the tongue of the wise brings healing." How can our words bring healing and help? How can they bring encouragement and strength rather than strife and difficulty?

A friend of mine opened an annuity for her son when he was a toddler that is supposed to pay him a substantial amount of money when he reaches retirement age. What a great legacy to leave her child, freeing him from the anxiety of wondering whether his savings will be large enough to support him when he's ready to retire. What if we had it in our power to do something similar for our own children? No matter what the size of our bank accounts, we do have that power. My father was not a man who always spoke positively. But one thing he said to me as a young girl has stuck with me, helping to shape the course of my life. "You can do anything you want to when you grow up," he said. I knew he was telling me that he thought I would find success in life. His confidence in me has buoyed me through many challenges. Similarly, we can look for opportunities to find something worth commending, especially in those closest to us.

Art Buchwald tells a delightful story about a friend who was on a one-man encouragement campaign in New York City. Buchwald was riding in a cab with him one day. When they arrived at their destination, his friend turned to the driver and said: "Thank you for the ride. You did a superb job of driving."

Noting the driver's astonishment at being complimented, Buchwald asked his friend what he was up to. "I am trying to bring love back to New York," he announced. "I believe it's the only thing that can save the city."

"How can one man save New York?" Buchwald asked.

"It's not one man. I believe I have made the taxi driver's day. Suppose he has twenty fares. He's going to be nice to those twenty fares because someone was nice to him. Those fares in turn will be kinder to their employees or shop-keepers or waiters or even their own families. Eventually the goodwill could spread to at least 1,000 people."

"But you're depending on that taxi driver to pass your good-will to others," Buchwald objected.

"I'm aware that the system isn't foolproof," his friend replied, "so I might deal with ten different people today. If, out of ten, I can make three happy, then eventually I can indirectly influence the attitudes of 3,000 more."

As the two men walked down the street, his friend compli-mented a group of construction workers on the quality of their work. But his campaign didn't end there.

"You just winked at a very plain-looking woman," Buchwald remarked as the two men kept walking.

"Yes, I know. And if she's a schoolteacher, her class will be in for a fantastic day."

Buchwald's story delights and amuses, but it also enlight-ens. We sense that his friend is right because we, too, have been cheered by strangers who treated us with uncommon courtesy or kindness. Wouldn't it be great to start our own encouragement campaign, extending it not just to strangers but to the people we know the best, those in our families, churches, and workplaces?

Learning to create peace with our tongues is a lifelong challenge, one that few of us will ever master. But that shouldn't stop us from trying. A fourth-century Christian by the name of John of Antioch was nicknamed *Chrysostomos* because of his eloquent preaching. History knows him as St. John Chrysostom, a name that means "Golden Tongue." Would that we would develop our own golden tongues, using our mouths to reflect God's truth and love to a world that needs his peace.

PURSUING PEACE

1. Paul Tripp says that we lose control of our tongues not because of the *facts* of a situation but because of the way we *interpret* those facts. Think of a time when this happened to you. Describe an alternate interpretation that might have been more accurate and more effective at helping you control your speech.

2. Describe an instance in the recent past in which you reacted to someone too quickly. How could you have slowed down your response time in order to have reacted more calmly and with greater wisdom?

3. What do you think is the best way to deliver a necessary criticism? Has anyone ever done this for you? If so, what was the result?

4. Describe ways in which you have learned to bring healing and encouragement through the words you speak.

Chapter 12

PRACTICAL
PEACE

> *If only you had paid attention to my commands, your peace would have been like a river, your well-being like the waves of the sea.*
>
> Isaiah 48:18

It had been a stressful day, preceded by a difficult week. Little wonder my back was aching. I gave thanks for strong hands rubbing out the pain. After the massage, the therapist asked if I was a swimmer. "Why, yes," I said. Delighted by the implied compliment, I concluded that I must have been in better shape than I had thought. Otherwise, how could she possibly have pegged me as a swimmer?

I decided to probe a bit. Perhaps the therapist would express her surprise that a woman my age was in such great condition. But when I asked how she knew, she simply said, "Oh, it's always easy to tell the swimmers. I can smell the chlorine!" With that, I slunk out of the salon, embarrassed by my short-lived fantasy of having morphed into wonder woman.

The truth is, had I been exercising more faithfully, I probably wouldn't have had to spend the money on a massage, nor would the stress I had felt been able to settle in the weakest spot in my body.

If we want to experience more peace and less stress in our daily lives, it makes sense to look at a few practical methods for doing so.

MAKE EXERCISE A HABIT

A practical way to reduce tension and anxiety is to make exercise a regular habit. Watching the *Wizard of Oz* with my children one day, I couldn't help but wonder if even the Wicked Witch of the West would have been kinder to Dorothy and Toto, had she only been keeping to a regular exercise routine. Seriously, regular exercise can reduce our anxiety and make us easier to live with. Unfortunately, many of us feel so exhausted by the demands of work and home life that we fail to carve out time for exercise, something that our forebears would not even have needed to consider. Though we can't time travel to another era to conduct studies on how our ancestors benefited from engaging in regular manual labor, we can once again learn something by looking at the Amish. Compared with average Americans, the Amish are six times more active than we are. No wonder a study conducted in 2004 indicated that the obesity rate in an Old Order Amish community was only 4 percent. Compare that to a 2009 study showing that a whopping 26 percent of Americans are obese.

The physical and mental health benefits of regular exercise

have been well documented. Most of us know we need it. But perhaps we have failed to realize the spiritual benefits of exercise. Rejecting a sedentary lifestyle in favor of one that is more active may help us become better disciples of Christ as our anxiety levels are reduced and we are able to respond to life's challenges with greater peace and trust. So get out there and chop that wood, take that run, sign up for a dance class, or join a health club. Do something you enjoy with people you enjoy so that you can take care of the body and mind God has given you.

BREATHE DEEPLY

Another practical way of easing your stress is to engage in deep breathing exercises. You don't have to be a Buddhist to recognize the benefits of breathing deeply, which can be explained by physiology. Chronic stress activates the sympathetic nervous system, which kicks into action automatically whenever you face or think you are facing an emergency. It releases adrenaline and other chemical messengers into your system, putting your body on high alert, preparing it for a fight or flight response. It's what caused my younger daughter, Luci, to jump with fright last night when I leapt out and shouted "Aaaagh" at her just as she rounded the corner of the stairway (bad mommy!). The sympathetic nervous system is great for dealing with emergency situations, but it's terrible for dealing with long-term stress. A chronically activated sympathetic nervous system disrupts the brain, causing depression, insomnia, and fatigue.

By contrast, the parasympathetic nervous system plays an opposite role. It takes over when the body is at rest. So when I looked in on Luci after she had gone to bed last night, I saw a young girl, who despite her earlier ordeal, was sleeping soundly while her body was quietly restoring itself. An activated parasympathetic nervous system can help your heart rate decrease, your muscles relax, and your lungs to take in more oxygen. Deep breathing helps to activate the parasympathetic system, thereby increasing your sense of calm and well-being.

GET YOUR SLEEP

Speaking of sleep, if you want to die young, make sure you don't get enough of it. Without the proper amount of sleep, we are at greater risk of major illnesses, including diabetes, cancer, and heart disease. Even our obesity epidemic seems to result in part from a chronic lack of sleep. Studies show that most of us need at least seven hours of sleep. Eight or nine hours are even better. There may be a variety of reasons why we are trying to get by on less and less sleep, but surely one of them is that we are up late watching television or playing video games. Exposure to the light emitted by television and computer screens can make it difficult to fall asleep. Another reason for our lack of sleep may be that we are depending too much on ourselves and not enough on God to make our lives work as we think they should.

DEALING WITH PETTY ANNOYANCES

Exercise, breathing deeply, and rest will help us to deal with the petty annoyances that come our way each day. The seventeenth-century writer Claude la Columbiére called these annoyances "tiny thorns." He writes, "All our life is sown with tiny thorns that produce in our hearts a thousand involuntary movements of hatred, envy, fear, impatience, a thousand little fleeting disappointments, a thousand slight worries, a thousand disturbances that momentarily alter our peace of soul. For example, a word escapes that should not have been spoken. Or someone says something that offends us. A child inconveniences you. A bore stops you. You don't like the weather. Your work is not going according to plan. A piece of furniture is broken. A dress is torn. I know that these are not occasions for practicing very heroic virtue. But they would definitely be enough to acquire it if we really wished to do so."

As Columbiére points out, these tiny thorns disrupt our peace, but they also present us with an opportunity. If we let them, they can train us toward greater peace and confidence. Most of us think that peace comes from avoiding discomfort, frustration, fear, and pain. But every life, to a greater or lesser degree, is fraught with such feelings. One of the keys to developing a greater sense of peace is learning how to deal with them. Feelings, of course, are neither right nor wrong. They just are. What we do with them, how we respond to them, is what matters.

So how to deal with all the tiny thorns in our lives? One way to handle life's innumerable disruptions, discomforts, and frustrations is by trying to escape them or by distracting ourselves from them. Sometimes our strategies work fairly well while at other times they develop into unhealthy patterns. We drink, we shop, we watch television — all to excess. Others of us respond combatively, blaming everything and everyone around us for the smallest offense. Inevitably, our dysfunctional strategies lead to guilt and not peace.

How should we approach the feelings we'd rather not have? We can begin by allowing ourselves to feel them. As we do, we can examine them carefully, looking for ways to understand ourselves and others better.

Are you feeling suddenly depressed? Develop some curiosity about what is causing you to feel that way. Did someone say something? Did you say something? What is creating the hollowness and sadness inside you? Sit with your sadness for a while rather than trying to stomp it out or run away from it. You needn't indulge it, but you do need to acknowledge it in order to learn from it.

How do you normally respond to uncomfortable or distressing feelings? Do you take a bath, go for a walk, get exercise, cook a meal, talk to someone, tell yourself to snap out of it, listen to music, pray, read, take medication, spend money, play video games, raid the fridge, complain, drink, mope, withdraw, yell? Whatever the negative feeling, whether it's anxiety, depression, anger, or boredom, you may have developed automatic responses as coping mechanisms. Taking a moment to be curious about them without being heavy-handed toward yourself can lead toward greater understanding and self-control, especially if you ask God to give you wisdom.

Try paying attention to the internal dialogues that are going on in the midst of these feelings. These will help you discover what is driving your reactions. I know a widow who finds holidays particularly difficult to face. She spends a lot of energy trying to engineer just the right experience for herself and her children. Recently, it occurred to her that her anxiety about holidays is closely tied to the story she tells herself. She had always believed that important holidays should be celebrated with extended family. She wanted her children to be enfolded into a wonderful experience that included grandparents, aunts, uncles, and cousins. But her larger family was either too far away or too preoccupied to join them. Once she identified the story line, entitled "the perfect holiday," she was free to respond in different ways. This year she let herself experience the disappointment of not being able to celebrate with her brothers' and her sister's families. But she rejected the narrative that her holidays would be ruined. Then she began planning a creative celebration that may provide new traditions for her own immediate family.

As you listen to your internal dialogues, ask yourself how you handle difficult events or problems. Do you tend to see bad things as discrete events or as permanent, all-pervasive problems? If your furnace goes out, for instance, do you conclude that it will only be a matter of time before the refrigerator goes on the blink and the roof falls down around you as well? Assuming you've taken reasonably good care of the house, you can reject that scenario and change the dialogue. But first you have to become aware that you are having such a conversation with yourself.

As you begin to investigate your feelings, reactions, and the stories you tell yourself, try to do so without adopting a critical attitude toward yourself or others. Ask God to help you remember that you are the child of a Father who both understands and loves you. Extend to yourself the compassion you have already experienced from him. Francis of Assisi famously called his body "Brother Ass," a term that blends self-deprecating humor with a certain amount of affection. Though Francis treated himself harshly, he later asked pardon from his body for the extreme forms of self-discipline he had subjected it to. Sometimes we make a similar mistake by judging ourselves too harshly, castigating ourselves not physically but mentally. The way forward is found when we simply accept the truth God helps us discover while believing that he will give us grace to become the people he wants us to be.

As we investigate the source of our negative reactions, we may also find that the Holy Spirit gives us greater insight into people who have hurt or offended us. Facing our own shortcomings may make us more compassionate toward the faults of others, helping us to understand why they act the way they do. Consider the woman whose negative emotions tend to be expressed as anger. Whenever she feels sad, anxious, or stressed, she gets angry. Worried her children will become sick if they are short on sleep, she yells at them to get to bed. Stressed by too many things to do, she lays on the horn when another driver cuts in front of her. If this woman can begin to understand her pattern, she can respond more effectively to the underlying emotions that are driving her angry outbursts. Later on, when her boss says something rude, she might be able to recognize that his behavior has more to do with his anxiety about falling sales revenue rather than something she has done to offend.

Running from uncomfortable emotions like fear, hurt, or disappointment is not a way to create more peace in our lives. Instead, these emotions move underground, where they gain a greater power to control us. If we can simply let ourselves experience them, they are more likely to pass naturally in and out of our lives instead of lodging in hidden places in our hearts.

Last week I took my children to the pediatrician for a dreaded immunization. I tried to explain that the best way to get a shot is to simply relax the muscle in your arm when the needle goes in. That way you will be far less likely to feel sore after the nurse extracts the needle. It's the same with fear. Fighting it too much increases its potency, causing us to suffer from chronic anxiety or explosive anger. We needn't indulge negative emotions, but we do need to give ourselves permission to experience them.

When my mother was a young girl, she had a recurring nightmare. In the dream she found herself ascending a steep stairway toward a door. With every step she became more apprehensive, terrified of what might lie in wait on the other side. Each occurrence of the dream heightened her fear. Finally, one night, she dreamed that the door opened, revealing a person at the top of the stairs. She doesn't remember who the person was, but she never had that frightening dream again. Similarly, facing our fears or hurt in the presence of God can greatly reduce or even eliminate their power over us. Remember that Jesus spoke of the Holy Spirit as the one who would be our Counselor (John 14:26). Christ has not left us alone to muddle our way though life. Right after promising that the Father would send the Holy Spirit, he said this: "Peace I leave with you; my peace I give you. I do not give to you as the world gives. Do not let your hearts be troubled and do not be afraid" (14:27).

STAY IN THE PRESENT

Sometimes our tendency to live in our imagination diminishes the peace we experience. Our minds stray from the place we are, the people we're with, and the activity we're doing, with the result that we fail to live in the present moment. Researchers at Harvard recently developed a smart phone technology that randomly sampled more than 2,200 people in order to discover how they were feeling and what they were doing and thinking at any given moment. After analyzing a quarter-million responses from this large sample group, they concluded that people think about what is *not* happening almost as much as they are thinking about what *is* happening and that doing so typically makes them less happy. Translation—a wandering mind adds to our unhappiness rather than to our happiness. Though daydreaming about pleasant subjects made people less unhappy than daydreaming about unpleasant ones, they were not as happy at such times as they were when focusing on what they were doing in the present.

Daniel Gilbert, a professor at Harvard and one of the researchers behind the study, commented on their findings: "If you ask people to imagine winning the lottery, they typically talk about the things they would do—'I'd go to Italy, I'd buy a boat, I'd lie on the beach'—and they rarely mention the things they would *think*. But our data suggest that the location of the body is much less important than the location of the mind, and that the former has surprisingly little influence on the latter. The heart goes where the head takes it, and neither cares much about the whereabouts of the feet."

I remember an experience I had while traveling in Europe. Fearing that I might never visit again, I spent hours taking photos of everything I saw, trying to record the experience on film. But I spent so much time behind the camera, trying to get the best possible picture, that I began to feel as though I were missing the whole experience. Looking through a tiny lens all day long prevented me from taking in the sounds, sights, and smells of an incredible continent.

Of course there's nothing wrong with daydreaming or with thinking about the future, but if we make a habit of letting our minds live in those places, our thoughts will wander too far from the present, and we will miss the opportunities that God is providing for us to serve and experience him right now.

Knowing their tendency to be anxious about what might happen in the future, Jesus advised his followers with these words, "Do not worry about tomorrow, for tomorrow will worry about itself. Each day has enough trouble of its own" (Matthew 6:34). Jesus wasn't urging them to be passive but to pay attention to what was important in the present. Likewise, it is only in the present that we have the opportunity to do God's will, fulfilling his good purpose for our lives.

THE PEACE OF FOREVER

Entire books have been devoted to the subject of how we can enjoy more peace and less stress in our daily lives. In this chapter I have only scraped the surface. What's more, practical ways for managing stress will take us only so far. These may work well for the average person dealing with average levels of stress. But for someone who is severely depressed or who is living in abject poverty or who is fighting a terrible illness, stress management techniques will fall woefully short of the mark.

Whatever measure of peace we now enjoy, all of us will benefit from learning to focus on what I like to call "the peace of forever." But doesn't this contradict what I previously said about staying in the present moment? And doesn't it sound rather impractical? Perhaps at first. But I believe that focusing on heaven is one of the most practical things we can do to infuse the present with greater hope and meaning. Praying through relevant Scripture passages, reading a book about heaven, doing a Bible study on heaven—all these can help us gain an eternal perspective on the life we are living now. No matter how difficult our circumstances may be, those who belong to Christ are headed for an eternity in which God's *shalom* is not something we taste for a while, but something that will characterize our lives forever. By exploring the peace of forever, we are merely remembering the last chapter of the story on which our lives are based.

In an address to the Southern Christian Leadership conference, Martin Luther King Jr. offered a wonderful prescription for hope when he said this, "When our days become dreary with low-hovering clouds of despair, and when our nights become darker than a thousand midnights, let us remember that there is a creative force in this universe, working to pull down the gigantic mountains of evil, a power that is able to make a way out of no way and transform dark yesterdays into bright tomorrows. Let us realize the arc of the moral universe is long but it bends toward justice." And because it bends toward justice, it also bends toward hope.

The peace we desire, the peace God promises, transcends whatever techniques we may employ to diminish the stress and tension of modern life. In the end, only a life that is surrendered to God will discover the *shalom* that he alone can give. Wherever you are on your journey, I pray that you will begin it with God, sustain it through prayer, and end it in peace. And this is my prayer for you, taken from an ancient Celtic blessing:

Deep peace of the flowing air to you,
Deep peace of the smiling stars to you,
Deep peace of the quiet earth to you,
Deep peace of the watching shepherds to you.
Deep peace of the Son of Peace to you.
Amen.

Pursuing Peace

1. Examine your exercise, breathing, and sleep habits. Is there something you can change so that you can reduce your stress and increase your peace?
2. Take a moment to consider any uncomfortable emotions you experienced over the course of the last week. Ask the Holy Spirit to help you understand what caused the emotions and how you might handle them better in the future.
3. Why is it helpful to focus on the present?
4. How does having an eternal perspective help bring about the peace that God promises?

Chapter 13

PEACE IN
SIMPLICITY

For God is not a God of disorder but of peace.
1 Corinthians 14:33

Several years ago, tabloids were filled with the story of Elton John's spending habits. Over the course of twenty months, the singer-songwriter reportedly spent $486,000 for flowers. When asked to corroborate this figure, Sir Elton simply replied, "Yes, I like flowers." A few years later a smiling John Travolta was featured with his wife on the cover of *Architectural Digest*. His Florida home boasted two plane pavilions, a 7,500 foot runway, and a taxiway strong enough to support the weight of his 135-foot 707 jet. "Travolta," the writer cheerily explained, "has always been dotty about flying."

It's easy to excoriate the rich and famous for their legendary excesses. But to be truthful, I loved peering into Travolta's private world. In fact I used to be an *Architectural Digest* junkie, which explains why I know about his crazy fly-in Florida home. Each month the gorgeous four-color spreads would captivate me, transforming me into a voyeur admiring the stunning designs afforded by extreme wealth. But the more I read, the more uneasy I became. How could I continue to celebrate such lavish lifestyles when so many people in the world lack even the basic necessities? I began to wonder whether I wasn't a little John Travolta in waiting. The only difference between him and me was that I had never been given the opportunity to live out my fantasies as he had. I cancelled my subscription.

Greedy bankers and government policy have been blamed for the housing bubble that launched what has been called the Great Recession. But perhaps they are not the only culprits. An article in the *Wall Street Journal* points a finger straight at television. "The cable network HGTV," it charges, "is the real villain of the economic meltdown. As the viewership reached a critical mass over the past decade—HGTV is now broadcast into 91 million homes—homeowners began experiencing deep angst. Suddenly no one but the most slovenly and unambitious were satisfied with their houses. It didn't matter if you lived in an apartment or a gated community, one episode of 'House Hunters' or 'What's My House Worth?' and you were convinced you needed more. More square feet. More granite. More stainless steel appliances. More landscaping. More media rooms. More style. You deserved it.

"If you had any doubts about your ability to afford such luxuries, all you had to do was look at the 20-something couple in the latest episode choosing between three houses. Should they go for the fixer-upper, priced at $425,000? Or the one with the pool for $550,000? What about the one with room to grow for $675,000?"

John Bogle, founder of the successful investment firm the

Vanguard Group, is the author of a book called *Enough: True Measures of Money, Business, and Life*. In it he tells the story of an encounter between writers Kurt Vonnegut and Joseph Heller that took place at the home of a hedge fund manager in Shelter Island, New York. During the course of the party, Vonnegut pointed out that their billionaire host made more money in one day than Heller had made in a lifetime of sales from his wildly successful novel, *Catch 22*. Unimpressed, Heller responded that he had something the hedge fund manager could never have. When Vonnegut asked what that might be, Heller responded, "The knowledge that I've got enough."

But just how do you define "enough"? Someone once asked John D. Rockefeller how much money was enough. His reply? "Just a little bit more."

THE DANGERS OF PROSPERITY

Prosperity can pose a clear and present danger to our faith. In her book *Practicing Peace*, Catherine Whitmire quotes one Cuban's response to someone who had asked whether it was hard to be a Christian in Cuba.

The man smiled. "Not as hard as it is in the United States." When his questioner asked why, the man answered, "You are tempted by three idols that do not tempt us. One is affluence, which we do not have. Another is power, which we also do not have. The third is technology, which again we do not have. Furthermore, when you join a church or a meeting, you gain social acceptance and respectability. When we join, we lose those things, so we must be very clear about what we believe and what the commitment is that we are prepared to make."

Prosperity can of course be good. It is good when people are lifted out of poverty. It is good when we have what we need. It is good to experience God's tangible blessings on our lives. But it is easy to succumb to the delights of a materialistic life, becoming mediocre and dull in the process. What's more, materialism steals our peace because it makes us anxious, frustrated, and unhappy. We are like dogs forever chasing their tails, as though pursuing life's greatest prize.

As Philip Yancey points out, "beginning with Adam and Eve's brief sojourn in Paradise, people have shown an inability to handle prosperity." Perhaps that's why rock stars and movie stars are often such parables of self-destruction. Compare pictures of Michael Jackson as a young boy with Michael Jackson as a forty-something and you will see what I mean.

Kelly Kapec points out that most people associate the biblical story of Sodom and Gomorrah with sexual perversion. But according to the prophet Ezekiel, there was another insidious problem that contributed to the downfall of these cities. "Now this was the sin of your sister Sodom: She and her daughters were arrogant, overfed and unconcerned; they did not help the poor and needy" (Ezekiel 16:49). Imagine, fire and brimstone raining down on your head because you were prosperous and yet gave nothing to the poor!

THE BLESSINGS OF ADVERSITY

In contrast to the dangers of prosperity, let's look at the unexpected blessings that adversity can bring. Chuck Colson spent seven months in prison for his role in the Watergate scandal. "As lonely and demeaning as that experience was," he says, "I have never regretted it. I can honestly agree with Alexander Solzhenitsyn, who wrote from the gulag, 'Bless you, prison, bless you for being in my life, for there, lying on the rotting prison straw, I came to realize that the object of life is not prosperity, as we are made to believe, but the maturing of the human soul." Likewise, we can learn to become thankful for economic hardships that redirect our lives to God. Sometimes something good needs to be subtracted from our lives before something better can take its place.

I remember chuckling over a cartoon that shows a man swimming in the ocean. The first frame shows only his head, arms, and feet as he swims along. The second frame shows him floundering on the sand after the tide has receded. What's funny is that the outgoing tide exposes the fact that he'd been swimming naked. A strong economy that slides into recession can do something similar. It can expose our vulnerabilities. Losing a job can make all the stuff on which we still owe money seem more like a curse than a blessing.

Lisa Gansky, an entrepreneur and author of *The Mesh*, a book about the sharing economy, says the financial crisis was our culture's "blue-dye moment." "The idea is you inject blue dye into a system and you can see the capillaries," Gansky says. "The stress of the Great Recession allowed millions of Americans to see the waste and the excess in their own lives more clearly." The recession galvanized many people to seek creative ways to make money and pay down debt and led to the creation of "sharing" websites such as Airbnb and RelayRide. Necessity, as they say, can be the mother of invention.

The Practice of Simplicity

In recent years, some have been drawn to the practice of simplicity — a positive discipline that counters the tendency to equate the good life with amassing as much money and things as possible. The purpose of introducing greater simplicity to our lives is not merely to avoid the snares of prosperity but to use our prosperity to accomplish Christ's work in the world. Simplicity is a positive discipline that helps us resist the cultural tide and reshape the direction of our lives so that we can become a blessing to others. When you put money in the offering plate or send a check to a charitable organization, you may be saying no to an expensive vacation so that you can say yes to educating children and feeding the hungry. Instead of simply succumbing to the values of a materialistic society, allowing these to determine the course of your life, simplicity can enable you to maintain a degree of freedom so that you can more nimbly respond to God's invitations, whatever or wherever these may be.

Paul warned Timothy about the dangers of pursuing wealth, saying that "godliness with contentment is great gain. For we brought nothing into the world, and we can take nothing out of it. But if we have food and clothing, we will be content with that" (1 Timothy 6:6–8). To twenty-first-century ears, Paul's advice sounds radical. Living in a materialistic culture can make it difficult for us to see how such values have crept into our own lives. To counter our cultural blindness, it's instructive to look at the values and practices of people who have led intentionally simple lives, people like the Amish.

LESSONS FROM THE AMISH

The Amish are famous for developing practical proverbs like the following that express the simple wisdom that shapes their lives:

- He who has no money is poor; he who has nothing but money is even poorer.

- We live simply so that others may simply live.
- Use it up, wear it out, make it do, or do without.

The Amish cultivate simplicity by keeping their priorities firmly in mind. For instance, while two-thirds of America's farmland is occupied by farms of a thousand acres or more, Amish farmers generally limit themselves to eighty tillable acres because that's the size that can be worked by a family using horses instead of heavy machinery. Their priority is to preserve and build family life, and they do that by setting limitations.

Contrast this approach to the one adopted by many Americans whose prosperity creates a desire for bigger houses and an appetite that results in an ever-expanding American waistline. If we are to know the peace that comes from simplicity, we have to begin to set limits on what we allow into our lives.

The Amish rely on the earth and the natural rhythms of nature to preserve them from the franticness that characterizes so much of modern life. David Kline, an Old Order Amish bishop from Ohio, says that "on a Monday morning, if you ask a farmer what he plans to do for the week, he'll look at you as if you're crazy. He knows that it all depends on the weather. I like that about farming. God makes us aware of our limitations through weather."

Ever wonder about those quaint-looking carriages the Amish ride in? Suzanne Woods Fisher points out that the "Amish are never to lose touch with earth, which is why buggies' wheel rims and other farm equipment must not be separated from the ground by a rubber cushion." Furthermore, traveling in a horse-drawn carriage necessitates a more leisurely pace. Instead of talking on your cell phone as nature whizzes by, you can focus on the beauty of a summer day or the spell of lightning bugs as they flicker in a nearby field. By staying close to nature, by respecting the weather and the rhythms of the seasons, the Amish believe they can more easily stay in touch with the God of creation.

THE GIFTS OF THE SIMPLE LIFE

Another countercultural group, the Shakers, have largely died out. In addition to a tradition of excellence in furniture crafts-manship, they left us with the classic song "Simple Gifts," written by Elder Joseph in 1848. This familiar lyric captures our longing for the peace of simplicity:

> 'Tis the gift to be simple, 'tis the gift to be free,
> 'Tis the gift to come down where we ought to be,
> And when we find ourselves in the place just right,
> 'Twill be in the valley of love and delight.
> When true simplicity is gain'd,
> To bow and to bend we shan't be asham'd,
> To turn, turn will be our delight,
> Till by turning, turning we come round right.

If the Shakers are right that simplicity is a gift that can help us to come round right, how can we embrace the simple life without completely withdrawing from the world around us? Three years ago, a graduate student named Christina Wall made it into the national media because of a master's project in which she challenged herself to live for thirty days with only the technology available to someone in her socioeconomic range living in 1950. For her, that meant no TV, no microwave, no fast food, no ATM, no credit card, no voicemail, no computer, no email, no cell phone, no dryer, no dishwasher. It also meant plenty of time for practicing piano, reading books, playing board games, and reconnecting with friends. It also meant money in her pocket. "It's not that I was a 'big spender' prior to the project," Wall said. "I would just fall into what I call the Target Trap, i.e., go into Target for some toothpaste, walk out of Target $150 later with some greeting cards, a small vase, some socks, trail mix, and that latest and greatest book I'd been meaning to read ... oops, I forgot to buy the toothpaste!" Holding cash in her hands, she said, made her much more mindful of how she was spending it.

During her project, Wall altered her eating habits and began looking for recipes developed prior to 1950. Though she couldn't bring herself to eat Chicken French Toast with Peas, a recipe she unearthed in an old issue of *Ladies Home Journal*, she did manage to eat more simply and to drink what she characterized as "liquid heaven," milk out of a glass bottle supplied by a local dairy.

After the experiment had ended, Wall made choices about what she would bring back into her life and what she would leave out. The credit card came back but the ATM stayed out. The cell phone was relegated to the glove box for emergencies. Doing dishes by hand got the thumbs up because she found it helpful to do a little manual labor once in a while. Television got limited to about one hour every other day. Playing piano, reading more books, and reconnecting with friends all stayed in.

Perhaps an experiment like Christina Wall's isn't practical for you, but it may inspire you to develop one of your own. Doing without television or cell phones for a week, for instance, might suggest ways to simplify your life. Looking more closely at the kind of gifts you give at Christmas might help you resist the kind of gadget crazes that make life expensive, fractured, and more frantic. Mind you, I'm offering this advice as a parent who needs to hear it herself. As always, the important consideration is one's priorities. If you want more of God's peace, you have to become intentional about finding it.

Though many of us admire groups like the Amish, we can't imagine embracing even half of their austerities for the sake of a simpler life. But one thing we can do is to decide to match our values to our lifestyle. That will help us resist the tendency to let worldly desires determine our course. Instead of piling up debt to get what we want, we can learn to wait until we have enough money in the bank. While we wait, we can learn to ask God whether the things we want are even things he wants for us.

TRUSTING GOD'S PROVISION

I graduated from college in the midst of a recession. Jobs were hard to come by, especially jobs in my field. Shortly before I received my degree, I remember attending a workshop in which prospective employers were invited to address students about job prospects. Though I hadn't expected a pep rally, I was unprepared for the doom-and-gloom scenarios that were presented. As I felt my confidence sinking, I had a sudden thought: "You don't need a hundred jobs, you only need one." I grabbed that thought because it felt like a promise from God. Indeed, two months later, I was offered an entry-level position in publishing, one that opened the door to my career. Years ago God began teaching me a lesson I am still learning: when I put my hope in him, he will supply all my needs.

Prior to the recent precipitous downturn, I paid lip service to the idea that God provided all I had and so therefore all of my money belonged to him. The truth is I spent money as though 90 percent (all but my tithe) was completely under my direction. It was only when money became tight that I began to learn that everything I own belongs to God. Now when money comes in, I praise him for every penny, acknowledging that it is his money to dispose of as he wants. "How should we use this money, Lord?" has become a question I frequently ask. Should I take that business trip? Or would it be a distraction? Should I send my children to public or private schools? Where do you want my tithe to go? Are there ways I could save money in order to give more? Should I save up for a new roof for my house or consider moving to a smaller home before the roof needs to be replaced?

I used to assume I knew the answer to these and other questions. Now I ask. Strangely, this change in attitude has brought greater freedom and peace. I no longer have to carry the burden of supporting my family all on my own. Now I realize that my role is to follow God faithfully, and his role is to provide. It's his money 100 percent — at least that's how I want to think about it.

Sometimes God might strip us of what we have in order to reveal who he is and the riches of what we have in him. Let me offer an example. What would you think if the president of the United States were to order a five-star general to dismiss 99 percent of his fighting force before meeting a formidable enemy on the field of battle? It sounds crazy, doesn't it? But that's exactly what God ordered Gideon to do. Remember the scene in the Bible in which Gideon and his 32,000 men are ready to take on the Midianites? Before they can attack, God tells Gideon that he has too many men for the job. So Gideon's force of fighting men is finally whittled down to a paltry 300. With this tiny army, beating all the odds, he comes up with an astonishing plan to defeat the enemy (Judges 6–8). Similarly, God sometimes strips us of the resources we think we need to live successful lives. For believers, success is defined not by *what* we have but by *who* we have—the God who is able to do far more than we could ever ask or imagine.

The story of Gideon is instructive for another reason. A fearful man whose courage is activated by an encounter with God, Gideon built an altar and called it *Yahweh Shalom*, which means "The Lord Is Peace." Gideon found peace through following the Lord faithfully.

Paring Down

A few years ago, blogger Dave Bruno issued the "100 Thing Challenge." The idea was to whittle down your personal belongings (not shared things like dining room tables) to a hundred essential items as a way of breaking free from the trap of American consumerism. Bruno believed that many of us are "stuck in stuff." He was certain that people who gave up their stuff for awhile would never want to return to a life of endless consumerism. Inspired by Bruno's challenge, Tammy Strobel decided to radically simplify her own life. Now she and her husband, Logan Smith, a doctoral candidate in physiology, live on her $24,000 a year salary. Having sold their two cars, they live in a four-hundred-square-foot studio apartment in Portland, Oregon, and travel most places by bike.

Three years after the start of their downsizing project, they are no longer saddled with $30,000 in debt. At first Strobel's mother called her crazy. Now she realizes her daughter is crazy like a fox, since she and her son-in-law have enough money to travel and to contribute to an educational fund for nieces and nephews. Now that Strobel is a freelance writer and web designer rather than a project manager for an investment firm, she also has more time to spend outdoors or volunteering for causes she believes in.

I have to confess that I am an unlikely candidate for the "100 Thing Challenge," nor do I cherish the idea of selling my car and living in a studio apartment. Those closest to me know that I am not a paragon of simplicity. But Tammy Strobel's example inspires me to envision how much more purposeful and enjoyable my life could become through greater simplicity.

For more than 350 years, the Quakers have been living a kind of spirituality that they call "plain living." Author Catherine Whitmire explains that plain living is *"a matter of spiritual intent, or an aim of the heart."* The early Quakers called this "staying close to the root." "Living simply," she explains, "means adopting a lifestyle that avoids the unnecessary accumulation of material items, or what Quakers have often referred to as 'cumber.' "

The thrust of simplicity is positive, not negative. Living plainly means making more room in your life for God. Here's how a group of Quakers characterizes the kind of life they are aiming at. "Outwardly, simplicity is shunning superfluities of dress, speech, behavior, and possessions, which tend to obscure our vision of reality. Inwardly, simplicity is spiritual detachment from the things of this world as part of the effort to fulfill the first commandment: to love God with all of the heart and mind and strength ... Simplicity does not mean drabness or narrowness but is essentially positive, being the capacity for selectivity in one who holds attention on the goal. Thus simplicity is an appreciation of all that is helpful towards living as children of the living God."

SIMPLIFYING OUR TIME

Author Wayne Muller points out that many of us have made a bad bargain by trading in our time for money. "The problem," he says, "is not simply that we work too much. We are paid in the wrong currency ... We need to seek instead a more fertile, healing balance of payments—some of our pay in money, and some of our pay in time.

"What if we were to expand our definition of wealth," he asks, "to include those things that grow only in time—time to walk in the park, time to take a nap, time to play with children, to read a good book, to dance, to put our hands in the garden, to cook playful meals with friends, to paint, to sing, to meditate, to keep a journal."

Clearly it takes courage and determination to live out what is essentially a countercultural discipline in a workaholic world. Simplicity has both emotional and psychological dimensions. In his book *Freedom of Simplicity*, Richard Foster says that we need to refuse "to live beyond our means emotionally. In a culture where whirl is king, we must understand our emotional limits. Ulcers, migraines, nervous tension, and a dozen other symptoms mark our psychic overload. We are concerned not to live beyond our means financially; why do it emotionally?"

The truth is that many of us wear busyness like a badge of honor. I am busy; therefore, I am important. Or perhaps we think the world will collapse if we are not there to prop it up. Though idleness may be the devil's workshop, surely busyness must be his stock in trade, creating countless diversions to prevent us from enjoying a life of peace or significance.

In order to live more simply, Richard Foster made the decision to accept only a certain number of speaking engagements during the course of a year. Once that big decision was made, he could say no with peace to even the most enticing invitations, believing that God had called him to limit his time on the road. In similar fashion, we can prayerfully survey our own lives, asking whether we can make a few practical decisions that will produce greater peace for ourselves and our families.

For instance, we could decide to restrain our spending by limiting or eliminating recreational shopping. Or we could combine forces with a neighbor to share a weekly meal. We needn't become Quakers or Shakers in order to enjoy a life of greater simplicity. We just need to start making a few sensible decisions that will obviate the need to make a thousand little decisions on the spur of the moment. Simplicity is a process. It doesn't happen overnight. It takes time to unwind a life built on consumption, reshaping our lives in the direction of greater simplicity and deeper peace.

Sometimes simplicity involves the discipline of waiting. Waiting grounds us in reality. When we wait, we admit that we are living with certain natural limitations. Paradoxically, it can also empower us because we realize that we have a degree of power in choosing how we want to live. Waiting gives us time to think, enabling us to resist the fantasy of runaway desires. One rule of thumb might be to postpone any discretionary spending over a hundred dollars for twenty-four hours. That would be a small step in taking control of our desire for more.

No doubt living simply is both a balancing act and a moving target. One person's simplicity may well be another's complexity. Though simplicity may be in the eye of the beholder, researchers agree that money can indeed make you happy—up to a point.

Having enough money to meet your basic needs provides a baseline for happiness. It's hard to be happy if you are barely surviving. New research is showing that once these needs are met, what you spend your money on can determine how happy you feel. For instance, people experience more happiness by spending their money on leisure activities such as vacations and concerts than they do on material goods such as couches and clothes. Why? Because leisure activities often connect us to others. The more and better relationships you have, the happier you will be. Also you can relive a vacation in your memory. It's much harder to relive a dress or a dining room table.

GENEROUS GIVING

I would argue that generous giving also makes you happier, pretty much for the same reason — it connects you to others in a meaningful way. Indigenous people of the Pacific Northwest have long observed this connection, which is evident in their festive ceremony known as a *potlach*. The main purpose of a *potlach* is to give away wealth to others. In contrast to modern, Western culture, family status in these indigenous cultures is determined not by how much you own but by how much you give away. Remember the widow of the Gospels who gave her last penny to the temple treasury? Jesus honors her by saying, "Truly I tell you ... this poor widow has put in more than all the others. All these people gave their gifts out of their wealth; but she out of her poverty put in all she had to live on" (Luke 21:3–4). Because of her generosity, which far exceeded the ideal of simplicity we are discussing in this chapter, her status in God's kingdom is great.

Another time Jesus instructed the crowds, saying, "Your eye

is the lamp of your body. When your eyes are healthy, your whole body also is full of light. But when they are unhealthy, your body also is full of darkness" (Luke 11:34). Behind the Greek text lies a Jewish idiom, which in Hebrew is *ayin tovah*, which literally means "having a good eye." Jesus was not talking about 20/20 vision or some kind of mental clarity but about being able to *see* the needs of others so that you could supply them. The opposite, *ayin ra'ah*, can be translated as "having an evil eye." A person with an evil eye has blinded himself to the needs of others, becoming grasping and stingy. According to Jesus, generosity is linked to light while miserliness brings on darkness.

Jewish theologian Abraham Heschel observed that "inner liberty depends upon being exempt from domination of things as well as from domination of people. There are many," he says, "who have acquired a high degree of political and social liberty, but only very few are not enslaved to things. This is our constant problem — how to live with people and remain free, how to live with things and remain independent." Heschel goes on to say that when ancient peoples wanted to emphasize something in their literature, they didn't employ italics or underlining. Instead they repeated it. Of the Ten Commandments, he points out, "only one is proclaimed twice, the last one: 'Thou shalt not covet ... Thou shalt not covet.'" To have less and to want less can be a path to freedom.

This principle holds true whether it applies to people, possessions, or food. Commenting on how good she felt after fasting from sugar for eighteen months, popular speaker and writer Lysa TerKeurst made an insightful comment. "Nothing," she said, "tastes as good as peace feels." When it comes to controlling our desires and bringing them under the direction of God's Spirit, we can all agree. *Nothing tastes as good as peace feels.*

PURSUING PEACE

1. Why do you think it's difficult for most of us to handle prosperity well?

2. What sounds appealing about embracing a life of greater simplicity? What sounds unappealing?

3. Quakers call the unnecessary accumulation of material goods "cumber." List three material things in your life that make you feel encumbered.

4. List three practical decisions that would bring greater simplicity to your life.

Chapter 14

WITH JOY AND THANKSGIVING

You will go out in joy and be led forth in peace; the mountains and hills will burst into song before you, and all the trees of the field will clap their hands.

Isaiah 55:12

Several years ago a neighbor told me about a bridal shower she had hosted in her home. Her daughter, Christine, was only three at the time. Christine's best friend was another small beauty named Momo, short for Maureen. The two little girls were always laughing or giggling over some shared mischief. But on the day of the shower they seemed perfectly behaved.

Angelic smiles graced their chubby cheeks as they handed out glass after glass of cool, clear water to the assembled guests. How darling they were! How helpful! It wasn't until the last guest had left that the truth came out. A suspicious older sister had followed the two girls, determined to find out what they were up to. She soon discovered that they had been grabbing glasses from the table, taking them to the bathroom, filling them with water from the toilet, and then serving them to the guests at the shower! That day many of the guests had washed down their cheesecake with a libation of toilet water.

I thought the story was hilarious, until it occurred to me that it had happened during a year chock full of babies and showers. I wondered if I had been there that day. I couldn't remember, nor did I want to. In any case, Christine and Momo's chicanery puts an entirely new twist on the old saying that you can either look at life as a glass half empty or a glass half full. By telling you the story, I choose to remember it as a glass half full, grateful for the laughter it still inspires, unless, of course, I am ill-mannered enough I tell it at a shower.

When it comes to experiencing more of God's peace, learning to become more grateful in the midst of life's ups and downs can make all the difference. But is gratitude really all that important?

THE MAGIC OF COMPOUNDING

Before we probe the answer to that question, I want to look at an investment principle that some have called the "magic of compounding." Despite economic downturns, we know it's possible to make huge sums of money by investing wisely over the course of many years. Say that you invest a hundred dollars at an average interest rate of 8 percent. In just nine years you will double your money. Without investing another penny, you will have ten times the amount of money in thirty years. A closer look at gratitude would seem to indicate that it functions something like compound interest when it comes to experiencing the peace God has for us.

For one thing, gratitude assumes that there is order and meaning in the universe, with someone at the helm. We are not mere atoms batting about in a chaotic world. Furthermore, the one at the helm is the same one who invites us to call him Father. Gratitude is an expression of our belief that God is sovereign and that he cares about us.

I have often wondered how my atheist friends can express their gratitude for something as simple as a day full of sunshine or a night crammed with stars. If the universe came into being by chance, there can be no one to thank. G. K. Chesterton called gratitude "happiness doubled by wonder." But it is hard to experience wonder in a life bereft of God.

What a contrast with the psalmist, who sings:

> *O my soul, bless God!*
> *God, my God, how great you are!*
>   *beautifully, gloriously robed,*
> *Dressed up in sunshine,*
>   *and all heaven stretched out for your tent.*
> *You built your palace on the ocean deeps,*
>   *made a chariot out of clouds and took off on wind-*
>   *wings. (Psalm 104:1–2 MSG)*

Thanksgiving is a persistent theme throughout the entire Bible:

> *Give thanks to the LORD for he is good;*
>   *his love endures forever. (1 Chronicles 16:34)*

The LORD *is my strength and my shield;*
  my heart trusts in him, and he helps me.
My heart leaps for joy,
  and with my song I praise him. (Psalm 28:7)

I will give you thanks in the great assembly;
  among the throngs I will praise you. (Psalm 35:18)

Enter his gates with thanksgiving
  and his courts with praise. (Psalm 100:4)

The ancient Israelites knew the value of gratitude. David, for instance, appointed Levites to give thanks to God at the moment the ark of the covenant was being brought into Jerusalem (1 Chronicles 16:4). Nehemiah assigned two large choirs to sing thanks to God when the walls of Jerusalem (the city's main defense) were dedicated (Nehemiah 12:31–43). There are even hints that thanksgiving can be a powerful force for peace. When heading out to battle, one of the kings of Judah once ordered a number of men to march at the head of his army. They had only one job—to proclaim their thanks to God (2 Chronicles 20:20–29). Remarkably, when the king arrived on the field of battle, he found it strewn with the bodies of his enemies. While his men had been thanking God, praising him for his goodness, their enemies had turned on each other and destroyed themselves. Thanksgiving, it seems, is not only a good defense but a good offense, sometimes creating peace by destroying our enemies.

Today many of our enemies are more internal than external. Fear shadows us. We don't have enough money. We doubt God cares for us. We suffer in difficult marriages. We've lost our connection with children who have gone their own way. Too often home is a place not of peace but of continual strife. It sucks the hope right out of us.

Instead of collapsing in the face of these enemies, we can take the offensive by turning our attention back where it belongs— squarely on God and his goodness. If money is the problem, you can thank God for all the things you do have. When relationships are painful, you can thank God in advance for the healing and restoration you hope for. Expressing gratitude in both good times and bad will remind you of all that God has already done for you. It will also help you to realize that you are not alone. You belong to a loving and powerful God, who is not indifferent to your problems.

A COMPLAINT-FREE WORLD

The opposite of gratitude, of course, is complaint. Habitual complaining creates a negative environment in which it is difficult to experience God's peace. A couple of years ago pastor Will Bowen challenged his congregation in Kansas City, Missouri, to wear purple bracelets as a way of monitoring their efforts to eliminate the habit of complaining from their lives. Since then, his organization, A Complaint Free World, has distributed nearly six million of these bracelets to people worldwide. Bowen challenges people to break their habit of complaining by placing a bracelet on their wrist. Every time they complain, they are to switch the bracelet to their other wrist. The goal is to go for twenty-one days without needing to switch the bracelet. It's gimmicky, but several people attest to the effectiveness of this simple idea.

One person reported that she no longer suffers from migraines since she stopped complaining.

Another person, a father from Arizona, says that every night at dinner his family discusses their failures and successes as well as ideas for how they might become a complaint-free family. The result, he says, has been "an increased sense of caring, happiness, and peace within our home." He goes on to explain that this effort has "added new insight to my understanding of parenting. I was raised to believe that a certain type of discipline was the only way to mold a child (such as spanking or yelling). Applying a complaint-free environment has shown my wife and me that our children will respond differently to a positive tone in our voice. They don't become defensive as they normally do when we raise our voice and speak in a negative, complaining tone. This has created a dramatic change in our communication with the children."

Another man, a beauty salon owner from Texas, decided to paint the break room of his salon purple. Across the wall he stenciled the words: "A Complaint Free World." Then he handed each employee a bracelet along with a book and CD about the program, promising a reward to anyone who completed the twenty-one-day challenge. The first day was fun. The second not so much. On Wednesday, three of his employees walked out, saying they no longer cared to work at a place in which management refused to confront problems. Troubled by their departure, the owner prayed that night about whether he was doing the right thing. As he prayed, he realized that these three people were his biggest complainers. Staff members responded to the news of their departure with the response: "Thank God they're gone; they were always so negative." After hiring three new employees who produce twice the revenue of the three who quit, he frequently gets pulled aside by customers who tell him that what makes his beautiful salon such a great place to be is the people who work there.

Convinced by their stories, I've taken to wearing my own purple bracelet. So far, I've managed to keep it on the same wrist for a maximum of two days, a pitiful record especially since I was spending the majority of the work day alone in my office writing. At one point I even complained about wearing the bracelet!

Benjamin Disraeli is said to have remarked that he felt an unusual sensation. "If it is not indigestion," he quipped, "I think it must be gratitude." Breaking the habit of complaining can be a first step in becoming a more grateful person. It's hard to see all the good in our lives while we are fixated on all the bad.

Habitual complaining is a dysfunctional way of dealing with difficulty, a way of rehearsing our grievances without making any attempt to resolve them. We think that complaining will make us feel better, perhaps because by doing so we are letting off steam or assigning blame for whatever is bothering us. But a habit of complaining simply reinforces our discontent, spreading our dissatisfaction to others.

GRATITUDE IN GOOD TIMES AND BAD

But shouldn't we be able to tell God and others about the things that are troubling us? Of course. Some people think that being a Christian means acting as though we have no problems. Just paste a smile on your face and act as though everything is fine in complete defiance of the facts on the ground. But this is lunacy, not gratitude. Jesus didn't come to earth in order to turn people into Pollyannas. He isn't asking us to pretend that life is better than it is. He came to heal us and save us and to restore our relationship with the Father and with each other. Honesty is essential for any healthy relationship.

Embracing the call to give thanks is not a call to hypocrisy, nor is it an invitation to paper over life's difficulties. Real gratitude is something far stronger. It's a call to proclaim the great truths of our faith whether times are good or bad.

Thanksgiving can pull our lives back into alignment with the truths we believe. We're thankful God made us. We're grateful for his forgiveness and his care. We're glad we have a purpose. Everything good in our lives is a gift from the God who loves us. The more we give thanks, the more thankful we feel. To praise God when we are in trouble is to light a fire in the midst of the darkness.

Mark Buchanan explains that "thankfulness is a secret passageway into a room you can't find any other way ... It allows us to discover the rest of God—those dimensions of God's world, God's presence, God's character that are hidden, always, from the thankless. Ingratitude is an eye disease every bit as much as a heart disease. It sees only flaws, scars, scarcity. Likewise, the god of the thankless is wary, stingy, grudging, bumbling, nitpicky."

Paul instructs the Thessalonians to "give thanks in all circumstances" (1 Thessalonians 5:18). Paul knew about "all circumstances." Just months prior to his letter, the Thessalonians had to smuggle him out of their city by night because an angry mob had become incensed by his preaching. Paul knew exactly what the believers there were facing. A few years later, he spoke of being beaten, imprisoned, shipwrecked, thirsty, hungry, cold, and naked (2 Corinthians 11:23–28). Paul's credentials as someone who suffered give him the right to speak to us about giving thanks in all circumstances. If it wasn't for what he endured, it would be so easy to disregard his advice.

Notice that Paul doesn't say to give thanks *for* all circumstances. He's not telling us to thank God *for* our difficulties. He is saying we should be thankful *in* the midst of our circumstances. I once heard a woman thank God for afflicting her child with a mental illness. I flinched when I heard her say that because it felt like such an insult to God's character. I don't for a moment believe that God afflicted her daughter with a mental illness. Rather, the girl suffered because she had been born into a fallen world. I think God grieves over our brokenness right along with us despite the fact that he is able to use it for good in our lives.

Rather than focusing on our circumstances, thanksgiving helps us transcend them by reframing the narrative. Paul could have taken his many afflictions as a sign that God had abandoned him. "Lord," he could have said, "I must be doing something wrong if so many people despise me." Or, "Why are you letting me get beat up and be thrown into jail just for telling people about you? You must hate me." But that's not how he reacted. Instead of focusing on his sufferings and building a narrative of complaint around them, he focused on God and built a narrative of trust around him. Paul's unshakeable trust kept his eyes focused on God's goodness rather than on all the difficulties he faced.

One of my children has trouble paying attention, which can turn ten minutes of homework into two hours. A few weeks ago she mentioned that she was looking forward to learning how to drive. But would it be a problem, she wondered, if she were to look around while she was driving? After all, there are so many interesting things to look at — houses whizzing past, people walking by, trees turning color. Keeping her eyes on the road sounded boring. She wasn't sure she could manage it. Of course I am in no hurry to put her behind the wheel of a car any time soon. Failing to focus on the right things when you're driving can be hazardous to your health. Similarly, failing to focus on the right things in your life with God can be hazardous to your spiritual health. Thanksgiving places the focus where it belongs—squarely on God and his goodness.

Most of us will never suffer the kind of hardships Paul endured. Our struggle to give thanks will occur in far more mundane circumstances. This morning one of my daughters left the house in a huff, angry that I had corrected her for something. Plus she barely made it to the bus on time, a frequent failing this year. Then came the phone call from school, "Mom, I forgot my lunch. Will you bring it?" I started rehearsing the morning's frustrations in my mind as I drove to school to deliver her lunch. Then I remembered that I was trying to follow Paul's advice to give thanks in all circumstances. So instead of reviewing my complaints, I began thanking God for his goodness and for the fact that he has a good plan for my child and for me. The more I thanked him, the more things I found to be grateful for: a crisp fall day full of sunshine, work I love, his provision throughout the year, how well my daughter was doing in general. Thanking him released me from petty annoyances that had threatened to ruin my morning.

SONGS IN THE MIDST OF SUFFERING

I remember how startled I was by a report I heard on the radio in the aftermath of the earthquake that struck Haiti on January 12, 2010. Watching the devastation and suffering in Port-au-Prince in those days was like watching a reality show on hell. In the midst of the chaos, three doctors and a physical therapist from Miami had joined hundreds of other health care workers to try to alleviate the anguish of the Haitian people. The four were stationed in a hospital tent that housed 125 people, most with devastating crush injuries. Some had huge holes in their skin. Bandages went unchanged, wounds were festering, and blood was everywhere. Air temperatures hovered in the nineties and mosquitoes filled the tent. As for the smell, it was like nothing they had ever experienced — a mixture of rotten flesh, urine, sweat, and stool. There was no running water and no toilets. Other than handing out pain medications, there was little the physicians could do to relieve the suffering. One health care worker explained that they had morphine tablets, which they placed in their patients' mouths "like a host."

"We all felt overwhelmed with worthlessness as physicians," one said. And then something happened that altered the atmosphere dramatically.

It was about 9:00 p.m. when a man with a guitar strolled into the tent. Pulling up a chair, he sat down and began to play. You could hear people beginning to harmonize. The health care workers alternate, as they tell what happened next.

"And then each row started to sing. The swell gets louder. Louder. And louder."

"As I open up the door, the sound is triple. Everybody. Every Haitian. Everybody is singing these words...."

"I remember panning my camera around and I just see this crowd of people singing and dancing in the center of the tent. People were jumping up and down. People with head wounds. People that couldn't get up because of their injuries, they were still singing and clapping along...."

"We turned to one of the translators and said, 'What are they singing?'"

"He said, they are singing, 'Jesus, thank you for loving us.'"

"It was like a knife hitting us. I mean from what we had seen. The amputees, the kids and how they sang that way. And the joy and happiness they had. It was a tipping point. Things changed after that.

"It's extremely humbling to be around a people that, in the worst time of their life, have in their hearts to give gratitude for what they have left, which is basically dust.

"I was so brokenhearted myself, just so tired, so sweaty, so fly-ridden, really, and in the process of pulling themselves up, they were pulling the nurses and the doctors up, giving us a great sense of hope."

Philo of Alexandria, a first-century Jewish philosopher, once said that "the grateful soul of the wise man is the true altar of God." Surely that day, the victims of Haiti's earthquake had constructed an altar to God in the midst of their unimaginable suffering.

Prayers of Blessing

In addition to telling the Thessalonians to give thanks in all circumstances, Paul advised them to "pray continually" (1 Thessalonians 5:17). This advice always puzzled me. How could anyone possibly pray all the time? That sounded like a recipe for crazy making. It wasn't until I began learning about the Jewish custom of offering *berakhah* or *brakha*, prayers of blessing, that I began to perceive Paul's meaning. Deuteronomy 8:10 advises the Israelites to "bless the LORD your God for the good land which He has given you" (Deuteronomy 8:10 NASB). In order to heed this Scripture, the Jewish people began offering short prayers praising God throughout the day. They would offer these from the moment they awoke until the moment they went to bed. Jesus himself would have said many such blessings.

This tradition has continued through the centuries so that observant Jews today pray on average at least a hundred blessings a day. Here are a few you might want to incorporate into your own life:

When you open your eyes in the morning:

Blessed are you, Lord our God, King of the universe, who gives sight to the blind.

When you wake up:

I am grateful before you, living and eternal King, for returning my soul to me with compassion. You are faithful beyond measure.

When you get dressed:

Blessed are you, Lord our God, King of the universe, who clothes the naked.

When you've survived an illness or danger:

Blessed are you, Lord our God, King of the universe, who bestows good things on the unworthy, and has bestowed on me every goodness.

When you go to bed:

Blessed are you, O Lord, Our God, King of the universe, who created day and night. You roll away the light from before the darkness, and the darkness from before the light. Blessed are you, Lord, who creates the evening twilight.

Blessed are you, Lord our God, King of the universe, who makes the bands of sleep fall upon my eyes, and slumber upon my eyelids.

May it be your will, O Lord my God, and the God of my fathers, to let me lie down in peace, and to let me rise up again in peace.

There are blessings you pray when you eat, bathe, study the Bible, receive forgiveness, encounter a beautiful person or a gifted rabbi, and even when you experience grief. The idea of thanking God even when life is difficult is that we are to love him with our whole hearts, which means we don't fence off the sad or mournful parts. But will saying so many formal prayers devolve into rote recitation? Will we forget what we are saying? Possibly. But it's equally likely that such continual acts of devotion will turn our eyes toward God, reframing the narrative of what is happening around us.

In *Sitting at the Feet of Rabbi Jesus*, Lois Tverberg and I comment: "Remember all the times your mother reminded you to use the magic words, 'Please' and 'Thank you'? She did it because she knew that this small habit has the power to instill attitudes of thankfulness and consideration. Likewise the habit of continually blessing God teaches us to be ever mindful of how much God loves us and how continually he cares for us."

In an effort to heed Paul's advice to pray continually, some early Christians developed short prayers called "aspirations." Augustine pointed out that the advantage of such prayers is that they are so short that they make it easier for us to maintain the concentrated focus that prayer requires. We can invent our own short prayers throughout the day. Something as simple as "Thank you, Lord, for giving me a place to live"; "Lord, I'm so grateful for food on the table"; or "Thank you for your mercy" will suffice. The point is to pray frequently and from the heart.

G. K. Chesterton once said, "You say grace before meals. All right. But I say grace before the concert and the opera, and grace before the play and pantomime, and grace before I open a book, and grace before sketching, painting, swimming, fencing, boxing, walking, playing, dancing and grace before I dip the pen in the ink." That's the attitude that should shape our own prayers as we seek to express our gratitude toward God.

THE GOD OF ABUNDANCE

At the heart of the biblical injunction to give thanks is the belief that ours is a God, not of scarcity, but of abundance. Theologian Walter Brueggemann points out that the Bible starts out with a song of abundance. Genesis 1, he says, "is a song of praise for God's generosity. It tells how well the world is ordered. It keeps saying, 'It is good, it is good, it is good, it is very good.' ... And it pictures the creator as saying, 'Be fruitful and multiply.' In an orgy of fruitfulness, everything in its kind is to multiply the overflowing goodness that pours from God's creator spirit."

Just how does God go about affirming this abundance in the lives of his people? For one thing, even when they are in captivity in Egypt, they multiply beyond Pharaoh's capacity to tolerate them. Then, in the inhospitable desert, God serves as their gracious host, feeding them manna for forty years. That this raggedy band of slaves eventually arrives at its destination is, Brueggemann says, "a wonder, it's a miracle, it's an embarrassment, it's irrational."

Haven't our parents always told us to count our blessings? What if that's a rather shrewd bit of advice and not a tired cliché, a strategy that will enable us to live a life of abundance rather than a life of scarcity? Gratitude, of course, does not guarantee a life of material prosperity, but it does affirm the truth of God's desire to treat us with tremendous generosity. By acknowledging the good things God has already done, our confidence in his future grace will grow. We can relax, opening our hands to the blessings he wants to give.

By contrast, thanklessness condemns us to living in fear. Instead of open hands, we become tightfisted. Closed hands cannot receive the blessings God wants to give. To be Christian and to be thankless is a contradiction in terms. It's like being a multi-millionaire who never reads her bank statements. Believing herself impoverished, she lives in a cramped, one-room house, terrified that she will run out of money and end up living on the streets.

Gratitude counters the belief that God either cannot or will not provide for us. That is true whether or not we are talking about material, emotional, or spiritual resources. God wants to give us what we truly need, whether it's money, peace, patience, wisdom, or faith.

In addition to expressing our gratitude through prayer and praise, we can express it by practicing generosity. By giving God at least ten percent of our income, we express our faith in his ability to provide for ourselves and others. We let go of our grip on all that he has given us, willingly sharing it with others. Generosity makes us more like the God we love. By giving food to the hungry, solace to the suffering, and shelter to the homeless, we reflect his image in the world. What's more, the practice of tithing can function a little like a vaccine, protecting us from the contagious power of greed. It is a concrete way of rejecting the narrative of scarcity and confirming our belief in God's abundance.

A Bigger God, a Bigger People

Giving thanks not only redirects our attention to God. It can also be an act of spiritual opposition, a form of spiritual warfare.

Why? Because an attitude of thankfulness resists the tendency of the world around us to cloak everything in negativity, enabling us to resist the pessimism that pervades the airwaves and dominates political discourse. It also helps us to reject the ever-present temptation to think that God doesn't really care about us.

Making thankfulness a habit inevitably affects our relationships because we begin to perceive others as among the biggest blessings we count. People who love us, who forgive us, who listen to us, who teach us, who pray for us, and who hold our hands when we need them to. All are expressions of God's care for us and all are to be thanked.

A reader did this for me yesterday. He began by explaining that God was opening his eyes to everyday blessings. In that spirit, he wanted to tell me that he had been helped by one of my books. Then he offered a specific Scripture passage as an encouragement for my personal and professional life. His words and the passage he shared were right on the mark, though he couldn't have known it. Nor did he know I was in the middle of writing a chapter on gratitude or that his note would reach me a few minutes before I walked in to a meeting with my publisher about future writing projects. It was a timely encouragement, an expression of thanks that might not have been given had God not been teaching him about gratitude.

Gratitude is expansive. It gives us a "bigger God" by enlarging our picture of his character. We realize that he is not limited in the ways he can work in us and through us. It also makes us "bigger people" by enabling us to reflect God's generosity to the world around us. As Eugene Peterson's wonderful version of the Bible puts it:

The world of the generous gets larger and larger;
    the world of the stingy gets smaller and smaller. (Proverbs 11:24 MSG)

If you want to experience the peace God promises, remember that gratitude can affect your life in the same way that compound interest affects your investments. Learning to be thankful regardless of circumstances will yield a larger, richer life, one that is securely grounded in God's goodness.

PURSUING PEACE

1. Why do you think thanksgiving is such a persistent theme in the Bible?
2. Do you think it is possible or even desirable to eliminate complaining from your life? Why or why not?
3. Think back on your experiences of the last twenty-four hours—morning, afternoon, and evening. Now imagine yourself reliving those hours. How might you give thanks—not *for* your circumstances but *in the midst of* them?
4. Describe a time in your life when you were able to thank God despite your difficulties. How did expressing gratitude at such a time impact you?

NOTES

Chapter 1: Where's the Peace?

Pg. 17: *Wendell Berry quote*: Quoted in Wayne Muller, *Sabbath* (New York: Bantam, 1999), 113.

Pg. 19: "*I am neurotic*": http://iamneurotic.com/2009/01/29/eri/ (accessed May 12, 2010).

Pg. 21: "*How to become Amish*": Uncle Amos, "Become Amish?" *Small Farmer's Journal* 17, no. 3 (1993).

Pg. 21: *Swahili for "white man"*: Mark Buchanan, *The Rest of God* (Nashville: Nelson, 2006), 196.

Pg. 22: "*can wreak havoc*": Robert M. Sapolsky, *Why Zebras Don't Get Ulcers* (New York: Henry Holt, 1994, 1998, 2004), 5.

Pg. 23: "*Let me just note*": Etty Hillesum, *Etty: The Letters and Diaries of Etty Hillesum 1941–1943* (Grand Rapids: Eerdmans, 2002), 535–36.

Chapter 2: Where Peace Comes From

Pg. 31: "*a religion of remembering*": Many of the insights in this chapter, particularly those about remembering, leaving Egypt, and maintaining one's relationship with God, are drawn from David Pileggi's unpublished sermon, "That I May Dwell among Them," delivered on March 28, 2009, at the Narkis Street Congregation in Jerusalem (www.narkis.org/Archives/Sermons/Sermons.aspx) (accessed April 2, 2011).

Pg. 33: "*maintenance*": Pileggi, "That I May Dwell among Them."

Pg. 37: "*Repentance is a realization*": Eugene Peterson, *A Long Obedience in the Same Direction* (Downers Grove, IL: InterVarsity Press, 1980), 26.

Pg. 37: "*is the action that follows*": Ibid.

Chapter 3: Peace Is a Person

Pg. 42: *puzzle of earth*: This story is recounted in Catherine Whitmire, *Practicing Peace* (Notre Dame, IN: Sorin, 2007), 127.

Pg. 43: *Elena Sanchez*: ASJ is the acronym for Asociación para una Sociedad mas Justa. This story is based on a news release issued on October 27, 2010, and posted on www.ajs-us.org/montes_abduction.htm#oct19 (accessed November 10, 2010).

Pg. 46: *Greek word for "peace"*: William D. Mounce, D. Matthew Smith, and Miles V. Van Pelt, eds., *Mounce's Complete Expository Dictionary of Old and New Testament Words* (Grand Rapids: Zondervan, 2006), 503.

Chapter 4: Peace in the Presence

Pg. 55: *"Dizler could have dismissed"*: Catherine Whitmire, *Practicing Peace: A Walk through the Quaker Tradition* (Notre Dame, IN: Sorin, 2007), 54.

Pg. 58: *"After this week"*: Amy Butler, "Anxious Presence," *Talk with the Preacher* (April 27, 2006) http://talkwiththepreacher.wordpress.com/2006/04/27/anxious-presence/ (accessed November 9, 2010).

Pg. 58: *"the trail of confidence"*: Quoted in David Cox, "The Edwin Friedman Model of Family Systems Thinking," *Academic Leadership Live: The Online Journal* 4, no. 4 (February 12, 2007), posted on www.academicleadership.org/emprical_research/The_Edwin_Friedman_Model_of_Family_Systems_Thinking.shtml (accessed June 7, 2010).

Pg. 59: *"If one family member"*: Edwin H. Friedman, *Generation to Generation* (New York: Guilford, 1985), 47.

Pg. 62: *"As Friedman points out"*: Ibid, 48.

Pg. 63: *"Scratch marks on their faces"*: Elbert Hubbard, *Little Journeys to the Homes of Famous Women Book Two* (East Aurora, NY: The Roycrafters at Their Shop, 1911), posted on www.kellscraft.com/LittleJourneysWomen/Little-journeyswomen02.html (accessed November 9, 2010).

Pg. 64: *"worldwide prison reform movement"*: Catherine Whitmire, *Practicing Peace* (Notre Dame, IN: Sorin, 2007), 45–46.

Pg. 64: *"nothing short of the Holy Spirit"*: Bill Samuel, "Elizabeth Gurney Fry (1780–1845) Quaker Prison Reformer" (August 1, 2001), posted at www.quakerinfo.com/fry.shtml (accessed November 3, 2010).

Pg. 64: *"Whenever I give workshops"*: Whitmire, *Practicing Peace*, 47.

Chapter 5: Peace in Scripture and Prayer

Pg. 69: *"Dr. Michael Burry has only one good eye,"* drawn from Michael Lewis, *The Big Short* (New York: Norton, 2010) (Kindle edition).

Pg. 71: *"Scion Capital"*: Ibid., Kindle 3763–67.

Pg. 73: *"In order to make"*: Virginia Woolf, *The Waves* (Ware, UK: Wordsworth, 2000), 135.

Pg. 74: *"As it would be"*: J. I. Packer, *Knowing God* (Downers Grove, IL: InterVarsity Press, 1973), 19.

Pg. 81: *"We're reading the story"*: Ann Spangler and Lois Tverberg, *Sitting at the Feet of Rabbi Jesus* (Grand Rapids: Zondervan, 2009), 68.

Chapter 6: Peace in Christian Community

Pg. 84: *Tara's story*: See Robert M. Sapolsky, *Why Zebras Don't Get Ulcers* (New York: Henry Holt, 1994, 1998, 2004), 108.

Pg. 86: *Amish on scooters*: Suzanne Woods Fisher, *Amish Peace* (Grand Rapids: Revell, 2009), 39.

Pg. 87: *Amish lower rates of heart disease*: Ibid., 67.

Pg. 88: *"Perfect community"*: Quoted in John Ortberg, Laurie Pederson, and Judson Poling, *Groups: The Life-Giving Power of Community* (Grand Rapids: Zondervan, 2000), 11–12.

Pg. 89: *"Our sense of self"*: Kelly Kapec, *God So Loved, He Gave* (Grand Rapids: Zondervan, 2010), 16.

Pg. 90: *"there are times"*: Dietrich Bonhoeffer, *Life Together*, translated by John W. Doberstein (New York: Harper & Row, 1954), 23. The actual quote is: "The Christ in their own hearts is weaker than the Christ in the word of their brothers. Their own hearts are uncertain; those of their brothers are sure."

Pg. 91: *"our grip on truth"*: Parker Palmer, *Let Your Life Speak* (New York: Harper & Row, 1990), quoted in Catherine Whitmire, *Plain Living: A Quaker Path to Simplicity* (Notre Dame, IN: Sorin, 2001), 143.

Pg. 93: *"Even when sin"*: Bonhoeffer, *Life Together*, 28.

Pg. 93: *"must bear the burden"*: Ibid., 101.

Pg. 95: *"confessing our sins"*: Ibid., 116.

Chapter 7: Peace in Sabbath Rest

Pg. 98: *"They are waiting"*: James Truslow Adams, *The Tempo of Modern Life* (Freeport, NY: Books for Libraries, 1931), 93.

Pg. 99: *John Ortberg and Dallas Willard story*: www.christianitytoday.com/le/currenttrendscolumns/leadershipweekly/cln20704.html.

Pg. 100: *"Good Samaritan Experiment"*: John M. Darley and C. Daniel Batson, "From Jerusalem to Jericho: A Study of Situational and Dispositional Variables in Helping Behavior," *Journal of Personality and Social Psychology* (vol. 27, No. 1, 1973), 100–108.

Pg. 100: *"to allow oneself"*: Thomas Merton, *Conjectures of a Guilty Bystander* (New York: Doubleday, 1968), 86.

Pg. 101: *space between logs*: Judy Brown, "Fire," www.judysorumbrown.com/poems/excerpts-from-excerpted-from-the-sea-accepts-all-rivers-other-poems/ (accessed September 29, 2010).

Pg. 104: *"reason for Sabbath-keeping"*: Eugene H. Peterson, *Working the Angles: The Shape of Pastoral Integrity* (Grand Rapids: Eerdmans, 1987), 49.

Pg. 104: *"Sabbath isn't eternity"*: Mark Buchanan, *The Rest of God* (Nashville: Nelson, 2006), 213.

Pg. 105: *"first holy object"*: Abraham Joshua Heschel, *The Sabbath* (New York: Farrar, Straus and Giroux, 1951, 1979), 9.

Pg. 105: *"The Sabbath"*: Ibid., 8.

Pg. 106: *"Six evenings a week"*: Ibid., 22–23.

Pg. 106: *"Shabbat comes"*: Ibid, xv.

Pg. 108: *"$2.44 per minute"*: Steven Erlanger, "Ultra-Orthodox Wield Power," *The Grand Rapids Press* (November 22, 2007), H6.

Pg. 108: *"for a long while"*: Mark Buchanan, *The Rest of God*, 106.

Pg. 108: *"I cannot think"*: Ibid., 45.

Pg. 114: *"It's precisely because"* Joseph Telushkin, *The Book of Jewish Values* (New York: Bell Tower, 2000), 18–19.

Pg. 114:*" reciting the blessing"*: Ibid., 19.

Chapter 8: Peace in the Midst of Suffering

Pg. 119: *"I would eventually"*: Leanne Miller, "Raising Cognitive Capacity," *Professionally Speaking* (September 2008), 35.

Pg. 121: *"Arrowsmith Program"*: For more information about the Arrowsmith Program, consult www.arrowsmithschool.org/

Pg. 121: *"In retrospect"*: Parker Palmer, *Let Your Life Speak* (San Francisco: Jossey-Bass, 2000), 99.

Pg. 126: *"The cross is the center"*: Joni Eareckson Tada and Steven Estes, *When God Weeps* (Grand Rapids: Zondervan, 1997), 135–36.

Pg. 127: *Letter to Audry*: Pam Woody, "Hours with Audrey," *Thriving Family* (January-February 2010), 44.

Pg. 127: *"There are a lot of things"*: Ibid.

Chapter 9: Healing from Hurtful Memories

Pg. 131: *"Miroslav Volf"*: The insights in this chapter are drawn largely from Miroslav Volf's outstanding book, *The End of Memory: Remembering Rightly in a Violent World* (Grand Rapids: Eerdmans, 2006).

Pg. 132: *"mid-level abuse"*: Ibid., 6.

Pg. 132: *"I wanted him"*: Ibid., 7.

Pg. 133: *"to remember is"*: Mark Buchanan, *The Rest of God* (Nashville: Nelson, 2006), 196.

Pg. 134: *"We are not just shaped"*: Volf, *The End of Memory*, 25.

Pg. 135: *"only truthful memories"*: Ibid., 75.

Pg. 138: *"Victims will often"*: Ibid., 33.

Chapter 10: Reimagining Our Enemies

Pg. 147: *"relationship with your enemy"*: John Paul Lederach interview on *Speaking of Faith* with Krista Tippett, July 8, 2010, posted on http://speakingoffaith. publicradio.org/ (accessed July 12, 2010).

Pg. 147: *"will prove fruitless"*: The analogy of Hamas's relationship with Israel is mine, not Lederach's. Additionally, I have taken the liberty of applying his point about imagining a relationship with your enemies to individuals as well as to groups.

Pg. 150: *"There are no devils"*: Angela C. Wu, *"As We Forgive*: An Interview with Laura Waters Hinson," on March 28, 2008, posted on www.cardus.ca /comment/article/26 (accessed July 12, 2010).

Pg. 150: "*Women and girls*": Christiane Amanpour, "Woman opens heart to man who slaughtered her family," May 15, 2008, posted on www.cnn.com/2008 /WORLD/africa/05/15/amanpour.rwanda/ (accessed July 12, 2010).

Pg. 150: "*We used machetes*": Ibid.

Pg. 151: "*There are no ethnic identity cards*": Wu, "*As We Forgive*: An Interview with Laura Waters Hinson."

Pg. 152: "*In his classic book*": C. S. Lewis, *The Great Divorce* (San Francisco: HarperSanFrancisco, 1946, 1973), 26, 29–31.

Pg. 154: "*In that moment, Wess received his calling*": Wess Stafford, "A Candle in the Darkness," *Christianity Today* (May 2010), 22–26.

Pg. 155: "*At age seventeen*": Wess Stafford, "Forgiving an Abuser," *Christianity Today* (July 2010), 43.

Pg. 157: "*generously, persistently*": For a more complete discussion of this passage and the technique Jesus was using in his response to Peter, see Ann Spangler and Lois Tverberg, *Sitting at the Feet of Rabbi Jesus* (Grand Rapids: Zondervan, 2009), 38–39.

Chapter 11: Taming the Tongue

Pg. 163: "*How many of you*": Joseph Telushkin, *The Book of Jewish Values* (New York: Bell Tower, 2000), 465.

Pg. 166: "*Swallowing words*": Quoted in Suzanne Woods Fisher, *Amish Peace* (Grand Rapids: Revell, 2009), 173.

Pg. 169: "*Didn't they know*": Paul David Tripp, *War of Words* (Phillipsburg, NJ: Presbyterian & Reformed, 2000), 18.

Pg. 169: "*The problem with the way*": Ibid., 21.

Pg. 170: "*in the heart*": Ibid., 94.

Pg. 171: "*When you're taking a vacation*": Ibid., 215.

Pg. 173: "*A parent must not*": Ibid., 47.

Pg. 173: "*Gentleness doesn't mean*": Ibid.

Pg. 173: "*The gossiper stands*": The actual phrase is: "The gossiper stands in Syria and kills in Rome" (Jerusalem Talmud, *Peah* 1:1).

Pg. 174: "*Blessed are they*": Quoted in Suzanne Woods Fisher, *Amish Peace*, 166.

Pg. 174: "*a status game*": Joseph Telushkin, *Words That Hurt, Words That Heal* (New York: Quill, William Morrow, 1996), 36.

Pg. 175: "*to find a way*": Ibid., 94.

Pg. 175: "*If you realize*": Ibid., 96.

Pg. 176: "*out of his own pocket*": Ibid, 99–101. Some of the dialogue in this story is paraphrased from the original for easier comprehension by non-Jewish readers.

Pg. 181: "*You just winked*": Quoted in Joseph Telushkin, *Words That Hurt, Words That Heal* (New York: William Morrow, 1996), 151–53.

Chapter 12: Practical Peace

Pg. 184: "*study conducted in 2004*": David R. Bassett Jr., Patrick L. Schneider, and Gertrude E. Huntington, "Physical Activity in an Old Order Amish Community," *Medicine & Science in Sports & Exercise* 36, no. 1 (2004): 79–85, referred to in Suzanne Woods Fisher, *Amish Peace* (Grand Rapids: Revell, 2009), 48–49.

Pg. 184: "*2009 study*": Bill Hendrick, "Percentage of Overweight, Obese Americans Swells," *Web MD* (February 10, 2010), posted on www.webmd.com/diet /news/20100210/percentage-of-overweight-obese-americans-swells (accessed November 17, 2010).

Pg. 187: "*Tiny thorns*": George Guitton, *Perfect Friend: The Life of Blessed Claude la Columbiére*, trans. William J. Young (St. Louis: Herder, 1956), 326, quoted and paraphrased in Bert Ghezzi, *Adventures in Daily Prayer* (Grand Rapids: Brazos, 2010), 59.

Pg. 192: "*in the present*": John Tierney, "When the Mind Wanders, Happiness Also Strays," *The New York Times* (November 16, 2011) posted on www.nytimes. com/2010/11/16/science/16tier.html?emc=eta1 (accessed November 17, 2011).

Pg. 192: "*If you ask*": Ibid.

Pg. 194: "*When our days*": Martin Luther King Jr., "Where Do We Go from Here?" delivered August 16, 1967; www.famous-speeches-and-speech-topics.info /martin-luther-king-speeches/martin-luther-king-speech-where-do-we-go-from -here.htm (accessed April 4, 2011).

Chapter 13: Peace in Simplicity

Pg. 197: *Travolta*: Nancy Collins, "Architectural Digest Visits: John Travolta and Kelly Preston," *Architectural Digest* (April 2004), 174.

Pg. 198: "*If you had any doubts*": Jim Sollisch, "Blame Television for the Bubble," *Wall Street Journal* (January 3, 2009), posted on http://online.wsj.com/article/ SB123094453377450603.html (accessed September 14, 2010).

Pg. 199: *Vonnegut and Heller*: Quoted in John Bogle, *Enough: True Measures of Money, Business, and Life* (New York: Wiley, 2009), 244.

Pg. 199: "*one Cuban's response*": Catherine Whitmire, *Plain Living: A Quaker Path to Simplicity* (Notre Dame, IN: Sorin, 2001), 111.

Pg. 200: "*Beginning with Adam*": Philip Yancey, "Forgetting God," *Christianity Today* (September 2004), 104.

Pg. 200: *Sodom and Gomorrah*: Kelly Kapec, *God So Loved, He Gave* (Grand Rapids: Zondervan, 2010), 42.

Pg. 201: "*As lonely and demeaning*": Charles W. Colson, "Commentary: I know what the Illinois governor feels like now," December 10, 2008, posted on http:// articles.cnn.com/2008-12-10/politics/colson.corruption_1_corruption-crime -spree-illinois-governor-watergate?_s=PM:POLITICS (accessed December 12, 2008).

Pg. 201: *"The stress of the Great Recession"*: Steve Henn, "What's Mine Is Yours (For a Price) in the Sharing Economy," NPR.org, www.npr.org/blogs/alltech considered/2013/11/13/244860511/whats-mine-is-yours-for-a-price-in-the -sharing-economy (accessed November 13, 2013).

Pg. 203: *"He who has no money"*: Suzanne Woods Fisher, *Amish Peace* (Grand
203: Revell, 2009), 21, 25, 51.

Pg. 203: *"on a Monday morning"*: Ibid., 72.

Pg. 203: *"Amish are never to lose"*: Ibid., 40.

Pg. 205: *"It's not that I was"*: Christina Wall, "Day 6—Results—Credit Card/ ATM," March 12, 2007, posted on http://retrochicky.blogspot.com/ (accessed September 15, 2010).

Pg. 209: *Tammy Strobel*: Stephanie Rosenbloom, "But Will It Make You Happy?" *The New York Times* (August 9, 2010), posted on www.nytimes. com/2010/08/08/business/08consume.html?_r=1 (accessed September 21, 2010).

Pg. 209: *"Living simply"*: Catherine Whitmire, *Plain Living: A Quaker Path to Simplicity* (Notre Dame, IN: Sorin, 2001), 15.

Pg. 209: *"Outwardly, simplicity"*: From the notes of the North Carolina Yearly Meeting of the Religious Society of Friends in 1983, excerpted in Catherine Whitmire, *Practicing Peace: A Devotional Walk through the Quaker Tradition* (Notre Dame, IN: Sorin, 2007), 96.

Pg. 210: *"What if we were"*: Wayne Muller, *Sabbath* (New York: Bantam, 1999), 101.

Pg. 210: *"to live beyond our means"*: Richard Foster, *Freedom of Simplicity* (San Francisco: Harper & Row, 1989), 91.

Pg. 213: *good eye and evil eye*: David H. Stern, *Jewish New Testament Commentary* (Baltimore: Jewish New Testament Publications, 1992), 32.

Pg. 213: *"inner liberty"*: Abraham Joshua Heschel, *The Sabbath* (New York: Farrar, Straus and Giroux, 1951, 1979), xiii.

Pg. 213: *"only one is proclaimed twice"*: Ibid., 90.

Pg. 213: *"Lysa TerKeurst"*: Lysa TerKeurst, "Nothing Tastes as Good as Peace Feels," posted on http://lysaterkeurst.com/page/3/ (accessed September 15, 2010).

Chapter 14: With Joy and Thanksgiving

Pg. 220: *"insight to my understanding of parenting"*: www.acomplaintfreeworld .org/stories (accessed October 6, 2010).

Pg. 220: *"Thank God they're gone"*: Ibid.

Pg. 221: *"If it is not indigestion"*: This quote is widely attributed to Benjamin Disraeli, though no source could be found.

Pg. 222: *"thankfulness is a secret passageway"*: Mark Buchanan, *The Rest of God* (Nashville: Nelson, 2006), 67.

Pg. 226: "*I was so brokenhearted*": Transcribed from "Six Months since the Quake," from the radio program *Under the Sun* from WLRN, produced by Kenny Malone and Dan Grech, posted on http://thestory.org/ (accessed July 13, 2010).

Pg. 226: "*the grateful soul*": As quoted in Joseph Hertz, *A Book of Jewish Thoughts* (Oxford: Oxford University Press, 1922), 283.

Pg. 228: "*Remember all the times*": Ann Spangler and Lois Tverberg, *Sitting at the Feet of Rabbi Jesus* (Grand Rapids: Zondervan, 2009), 98. For a more thorough treatment of the subject of blessings, see chapter 7.

Pg. 229: "*You say grace*": G. K. Chesterton, quoted in Frederich Buechner, *Speak What We Feel* (San Francisco: HarperCollins, 2001), 119. Buechner notes that Chesterton emerged from a kind of "personal nightmare" at the age of twenty and entered a period in his life in which he liked to call himself "always perfectly happy." According to Buechner, the quote was a "random piece" drawn from a notebook that Chesterton kept at the time. "Having been given back his life and sanity," Buechner comments, "he was filled with both an enormous sense of thankfulness and an enormous need for someone or something to thank."

Pg. 229: "*is a song of praise*": Walter Brueggemann, "The Liturgy of Abundance, the Myth of Scarcity," *Christian Century* (March 24–31, 1999), 342.

Pg. 229: "*a wonder*": Ibid.

Printed in the USA
CPSIA information can be obtained
at www.ICGtesting.com
LVHW030711050824
787165LV00011B/109

9 780310 320142